The Startup Playbook: A Step-by-Step Guide to Launching Your Business

New York City Books
www.nycitybooks.com

217 Peace Pipe Way
Georgetown TX 78628 USA

Printed in the United States of America

Publisher's Cataloging-in-Publication data
Arat, Mel
The Startup Playbook:
A Step-by-Step Guide to Launching Your Business

ISBN: 9798398484861
LCCN: 2023908814

The Startup Playbook:

A Step-by-Step Guide to Launching Your Business

Mel ARAT

New York City Books

"Mel Arat's Startup Playbook is a game-changer for aspiring entrepreneurs. His step-by-step guide provides invaluable insights and actionable strategies to navigate the complex world of startups. If you're looking for a comprehensive and practical resource to kickstart your entrepreneurial journey, look no further than The Startup Playbook." - **Hakan Turgut, Founder and CEO Mettleflex**

Mel Arat's insights are backed by real-world examples and practical advice, making it a must-read for anyone looking to turn their business idea into a thriving reality."
Henry Moodie, Author of 4 Days and 10 Steps to Greater Success According to Science

Entrepreneur's Dream

Entrepreneur's dream, ignited fire's gleam,
Unleash passion's flow, where possibilities grow.

Challenges embraced, setbacks interlaced,
Tribe of inspiration, together in creation.

Innovate, disrupt, leave a lasting impact,
Dare to dream, future's beacon, attract.

Journey unfolds, courage guides, stories told, Entrepreneur's mark, spirit shines, bold.
Mel Arat

CONTENTS

Introduction

"Don't worry about failure, you have to be right once."
Drew Houston,
Co-founder of Dropbox

This book is designed to guide and assist you in building your startup. If you have a burning desire to start a business, but you are not sure which idea to pursue, this book will help you to crystallize your thoughts and create a well-crafted plan to turn your dream into a reality.

In our daily lives, we often observe problems as customers and have insights into how we can improve an existing business service or create a new one. However, we may not know how to bring our ideas to life. This book will provide a step-by-step approach to help you make deliberate, logical decisions about every major aspect of your business without skipping anything substantial.

Unlike a traditional business plan that starts with an executive summary, this book emphasizes a thought process that occurs in relation to the problems of the customer and solutions for these problems. It begins with finding and making the business idea lucid, then developing a value proposition, and later addressing marketing, production, operation, financial, corporate philosophy, and people strategy problems.

The book's goal is to minimize waste of resources such as money, time, and human power during the startup stage by giving the readers practical guidelines and exercises to build their businesses brick-by-brick. Each chapter of the book provides conceptual explanations and brief guidelines about the relevant stage of the business. After each concept, there is a template for creating ideas and making decisions. By using the worksheets throughout the book, the reader becomes an entrepreneur, making choices to build his/her business.

Ultimately, this book aims to help you protect yourself from making mistakes, keep costs low, and give your customers exactly what they need while standing out in the market. So, take your business idea, turn it into a picture of what it will look like in your mind, and paint it into reality through the pages of this book.

The terms "startup founder" and "entrepreneur" are often used interchangeably, but they actually have different meanings. An entrepreneur is someone who seeks out business opportunities and profits. They are primarily interested in the profitability of the business and its potential for growth. For example, a chef who opens a restaurant is an entrepreneur who is focused on making it profitable as quickly as possible.

In contrast, a startup founder is someone who wants to create a business that will have a significant impact on people's lives. They are driven by a desire to build a company that will provide innovative products or services and generate substantial profits in the future. While startup founders also seek funding, they are interested in building a business rather than just selling it. However, it's important for startup founders to consider their exit strategy from the beginning, and the book includes a chapter on this topic.

The book takes a systematic approach that can be used by both startup founders and entrepreneurs. It provides helpful information and worksheets from the initial idea stage all the way to the exit strategy. It serves as a roadmap for those who want to start their own business.

"The Startup Playbook: A Step-by-Step Guide to Launching Your Business" is a critically important book for anyone looking to start or grow a business. This comprehensive guide provides readers with practical advice and easy-to-use templates for every step of the startup process.

Chapter 1, "From Idea to Reality: A Guide to Finding Your Business Niche," provides guidance on how to identify a profitable and sustainable business niche. This chapter helps readers conduct market research, identify gaps in the market, and develop a unique value proposition for their business.

In chapter 2, "The Art of Choosing: Selecting the Right Business Idea for You," readers learn how to evaluate business ideas and choose the one that's right for them. This chapter provides guidance on assessing the feasibility and potential profitability of business ideas, as well as evaluating personal strengths and interests to find the best fit.

Chapter 3, "Customer Solutions: How to Identify and Solve Problems for Your Market," teaches readers how to understand their target customers and develop solutions to address their problems. This chapter provides guidance on conducting market research, identifying customer pain points, and developing products or services that meet their needs.

Chapter 4, "The Power of Proposition: Building a Business Model with Value," helps readers create a compelling value proposition for their business. This chapter provides guidance on developing a business model that creates value for customers and generates revenue for the business.

In chapter 5, "Stand Out: Positioning Your Business in a Competitive Market," readers learn how to differentiate their business from the competition, build a strong brand identity, and develop a unique selling proposition.

Chapter 6, "Starting Small: The Minimum Viable Product Approach," teaches readers how to apply the minimum viable product approach to launching their business. This chapter provides guidance on building a product or service with minimal features, testing it with early adopters, and refining it based on customer feedback.

In chapter 7, "Competing to Win: SWOT Analysis and Competitive Strategy," readers learn how to assess the competitive landscape of their market and develop a winning strategy. This chapter provides guidance on conducting a SWOT analysis to assess strengths, weaknesses, opportunities, and threats, and developing a strategy that sets the business apart from the competition.

Chapter 8, "The Marketing Advantage: Creating an Effective Plan for Your Business," teaches readers how to create an effective marketing plan for their business. This chapter provides guidance on identifying the target audience, developing a messaging strategy, and using various marketing channels to reach and engage customers.

In chapter 9, "The Supply Chain Solution: Managing Your Business's Resources," readers learn how to manage the resources of their business, including inventory, suppliers, and logistics. This chapter provides guidance on optimizing the supply chain to reduce costs, improve efficiency, and provide a better customer experience.

Chapter 10, "Vision and Strategy: Developing Your Business Plan for Success," helps readers develop a comprehensive business plan that sets a clear vision and strategy for the business. This chapter provides guidance on defining the mission, values, and goals of the business and creating a roadmap for achieving them.

Chapter 11, "Corporate Culture: Building Your Business Philosophy and Values," teaches readers the importance of corporate culture and how to build a strong and positive one for their business. This chapter provides guidance on defining the company's philosophy and values and creating a culture that aligns with them.

Chapter 12, "Creating Your Identity: Branding and Marketing Your Business," provides guidance on building a strong brand identity and effectively marketing the business. This chapter teaches readers how to develop a brand identity that reflects their values and resonates with their target audience, and use various marketing channels to reach and engage them.

Chapter 13, "Building Your Team: Strategies for Attracting and Retaining Talent," teaches readers how to build a strong and effective team for their business. This chapter provides guidance on defining roles and responsibilities, identifying key competencies, and attracting and retaining top talent.

Chapter 14, "Pitch Perfect: Crafting a Compelling Business Proposal," helps readers create a compelling business proposal that effectively communicates their vision and value proposition. This chapter provides guidance on developing a pitch that resonates with investors, partners, and other stakeholders, and presenting it in a clear and compelling way.

Chapter 15, "Financial Forecasting: How to Create Accurate Projections for Your Business," teaches readers how to create accurate financial projections for their business. This chapter provides guidance on forecasting revenue, expenses, and cash flow, and using financial projections to make informed business decisions.

Chapter 16, "Business Structure: Choosing the Right Legal Organization Form," helps readers choose the right legal structure for their business. This chapter provides guidance on evaluating the pros and cons of different legal structures, such as sole proprietorship, partnership, LLC, and corporation, and selecting the one that best suits the business's needs.

Chapter 17, "The End Game: Planning for Succession and Exit Strategies in Business," teaches readers how to plan for the long-term success of their business. This chapter provides guidance on developing a succession plan to ensure a smooth transition of leadership, as well as exit strategies for selling the business or passing it on to the next generation. By the end of this chapter, readers will have a clear understanding of how to build a successful and sustainable business that can withstand the test of time.

1 From Idea to Reality: A Guide to Finding Your Business Niche

You can't use up creativity. The more you use, the more you have.
Maya Angelou
Author

1.1. The business idea

Having a business idea is a corner stone of the start-up process.[1] Entrepreneurs come in different forms. Some have a clear business idea and are eager to dive into it. Others may have an overwhelming desire to start a business but lack a concrete plan to bring it to fruition. If you fall into the latter group, this chapter is designed specifically for you. It provides a range of worksheets to help inspire new business ideas and guide you through the process of developing them.

Use the exercises in this chapter to generate innovative and viable business ideas. Even if you already have a solid idea in mind, this chapter can still offer fresh perspectives and insights that may help you refine your concept and take your business to the next level.

EXERCISES
- Solve an existing problem
- Solve a future problem
- Create new solutions to basic needs
- Help people save money
- Find a solution to make people's lives easy
- Make things and chores more entertaining
- Make products smart
- Combine different products
- Turn your hobby into a business
- Sell an experience

Upon completing these exercises, you will be required to select a business idea and utilize it as the focus of your work throughout the rest of the book.

---

[1] Woźniak, Dariusz, and Sokołowska-Woźniak, Justyna. Innovation, Entrepreneurship and Psychological Traits as Factors Influencing Productivity. Polonya, Fundation for the Dissemination of Knowledge and Science "Cognitione", 2018.

1.2. Solve an existing problem

Life is full of challenges and obstacles that can be viewed as opportunities for entrepreneurial ventures. Every problem or difficulty that you encounter has the potential to become a source of inspiration for a new business idea. By taking a step back and scanning your life, you can identify the issues that you are most passionate about solving. Similarly, paying close attention to the questions and problems faced by others within your organization or community can also be an excellent way to uncover new business opportunities. In fact, addressing the needs of others can be a particularly effective strategy for building a successful and sustainable business. With the right mindset, any difficulty or challenge can be transformed into a viable business idea.

Problem finding appears to be a crucial component of creativity, and what is more, it can be observed and assessed with satisfactory reliability and validity.[2] In the realm of entrepreneurship, problems serve as catalysts that generate tensions and stimulate the entrepreneurial mind to think critically and creatively. It is through the process of problem-solving that entrepreneurs strive to resolve these tensions and bring about innovative solutions. As a problem is successfully addressed and resolved, the entrepreneurial thinking process can evolve, adapt, and shift its focus to new challenges and opportunities.

Problem, Traditional Solution and Business Idea with a New Solution

For many people, counting calories can be a challenging and time-consuming task. While the traditional solution is to write down everything you eat, this method can be cumbersome and often leads to inaccuracies. That's why a new and innovative business idea is to create a smartphone app that utilizes image recognition technology to accurately count calories in real-time. By simply taking a picture of your food, the app can provide an instant and accurate readout of the number of calories consumed, making it easier for individuals to manage their diets and achieve their health goals. This app could be a game-changer for people who are looking to improve their health and fitness in a convenient and accessible way.

Many parents and students struggle with the challenge of achieving academic success in school. While private tutoring has long been a traditional solution to this problem, it can be expensive and inconvenient. That's why a new and innovative business idea is to offer online private tutoring, which can provide students with the

---

[2] Getzels, Jacob W., and Mihaly Csikszentmihalyi. "From problem solving to problem finding." *Perspectives in creativity*. Routledge, 2017. 90-116.

individualized attention they need to excel academically in a convenient and cost-effective manner. This online platform can connect students with expert tutors who can provide tailored lessons and feedback, allowing them to improve their grades and achieve their academic goals from the comfort of their own homes. By harnessing the power of technology, this business idea can revolutionize the way students approach learning and achieve academic success.

Transportation costs can be a significant expense for many corporations, and reducing these costs is essential for maintaining profitability. While traditional solutions such as buying fuel-efficient trucks can be effective, they often fail to fully address the issue. That's why a new and innovative business idea is to develop software that can optimize the routes of trucks, allowing corporations to transport goods more efficiently and cost-effectively. By using advanced algorithms and real-time data, this software can identify the most efficient routes and minimize fuel consumption, reducing transportation costs and improving overall profitability. This business idea has the potential to revolutionize the transportation industry and help corporations operate more sustainably and efficiently.

To generate new and innovative business ideas, it's important to be observant and attentive to the problems that exist in the world around us. Take a few moments to identify specific issues that you have observed, and then analyze the traditional solutions that are currently being used to address these problems. From there, challenge yourself to come up with alternative solutions that could lead to new and innovative business ideas. By thinking outside the box and exploring new possibilities, you can develop unique and valuable solutions that have the potential to transform industries and improve people's lives. So, take some time to observe, analyze, and innovate, and you may be surprised at the business opportunities that emerge.

Exercise
- How would you describe the existing problem that you have observed?
- What are the traditional solutions that have been offered to address this problem?
- What new business ideas can you come up with to provide a more innovative and effective solution?

1.3. Solve a future problem

In today's fast-paced world, change is the only constant. The recognition and development of new opportunities are at the heart of entrepreneurship.[3] Every day, new technologies and practices are introduced, creating new opportunities for entrepreneurs and businesses. With each new technology comes the potential for innovative new products and services that can meet the evolving needs of consumers. For example, when a new smartphone is launched, there is a sudden need for complementary products such as cases, chargers, and apps. By staying attuned to these changes and opportunities, entrepreneurs can identify gaps in the market and develop new and innovative solutions that can address the evolving needs of consumers. So, in a world that is constantly changing, it's essential to stay alert and open to new opportunities that can drive success and growth.

Exercise
- How would you describe some of the latest technologies or practices of today?
- What are the problems or opportunities that these new technologies/practices present?
- How can you leverage the problems or opportunities presented by emerging technologies to develop innovative and impactful business ideas?

---

[3] Tang, Jintong, K. Michele Micki Kacmar, and Lowell Busenitz. "Entrepreneurial alertness in the pursuit of new opportunities." *Journal of business venturing* 27.1 (2012): 77-94.

1.4. Create new solutions for basic needs

Our fundamental needs are universal[4], ranging from the need for shelter, sleep, and communication to education. While the basic needs remain constant, the solutions to address them are continuously evolving.

For instance, the concept of shelter has evolved over time from basic homes and hotels to the introduction of Airbnb in 2008. Airbnb offers a modern, home-based and affordable solution for travelers. However, a similar service for eating at home is yet to be established. This presents an opportunity to think outside the box and create new solutions to meet this basic need. By leveraging emerging technologies and innovative business models, entrepreneurs can develop new and exciting ways to provide convenient, affordable and high-quality food solutions for people in their homes.

Exercise
- What are some examples of basic needs that are commonly faced by individuals and communities?
- What are some of the traditional solutions that have been used to address these basic needs?
- What are some new and innovative solutions that have emerged to address these basic needs, and how do they compare to traditional solutions?

---

[4] McLeod, Stephen. "Absolute biological needs." *Bioethics* 28.6 (2014): 293-301.

1.5. Help people save money

Helping people save money is a goal that resonates with many individuals. By finding innovative solutions that can reduce costs, entrepreneurs can develop successful and growing businesses. One way to achieve this is by promoting the use of energy-saving or low-energy devices, which can help cost conscious people to reduce their energy bills over time. Additionally, collective or bulk purchasing programs can also offer significant cost savings for consumers, enabling them to purchase essential products and services at a lower price point.[5] By focusing on these types of solutions, entrepreneurs can help people save money and drive success in their businesses.

An example of a product or service that typically has a regular price is music CDs. However, with the introduction of new methods and technologies, the cost of accessing music has been significantly reduced. For instance, new product or service models based on music streaming have emerged, including popular platforms such as iTunes, Spotify, and Pandora. By leveraging technology to provide access to a wide range of music at an affordable cost, these platforms have transformed the music industry and enabled millions of people to enjoy their favorite music without breaking the bank. As a result, entrepreneurs should look for similar opportunities to develop innovative new business models that can help consumers save money while still enjoying high-quality products and services.

Designer clothes are an example of a product or service that often comes with a high price tag. However, there are ways to reduce these costs by leveraging new methods and technologies. One approach is to make contracts with designers to sell their past-season items online, which can help to clear inventory and reduce costs for both the designers and consumers. Another innovative solution is to develop a new product or service model that focuses on selling designer clothes online at more affordable prices. By streamlining supply chains and using digital platforms to connect with customers, entrepreneurs can offer high-quality designer clothes at prices that are accessible to a wider range of consumers. These types of solutions have the potential to disrupt the traditional fashion industry and create new opportunities for innovative businesses.

---

[5] Karmarkar, Uma R., Baba Shiv, and Brian Knutson. "Cost conscious? The neural and behavioral impact of price primacy on decision making." *Journal of Marketing Research* 52.4 (2015): 467-481.

—

Exercise
- What are some examples of products or services that are typically associated with regular pricing?
- What are some methods or technologies that can be used to reduce the cost of these products or services?
- What are some innovative new product or service models that focus on saving and reducing costs, and how do they compare to traditional approaches?

1.6. Find a solution to make people's lives easier

People often gravitate towards simple solutions that can make their lives easier and more convenient. This is evident in the evolution of everyday items, such as the replacement of wooden carpentry pencils with mechanical pencils that eliminated the need for sharpeners, or the introduction of frozen foods that made meal preparation easier for many households. Despite the many technological advancements and innovations, there are still many complex challenges that people face, such as changing a flat tire or relocating to a new city, that present unique business opportunities. There are also niche groups looking for easier solutions. Visually impaired individuals require accessible solutions to make shopping easier. [6] By developing simple, effective solutions that can help to address these types of challenges, entrepreneurs can create value for their customers and drive success in their businesses.

Another example, selling unnecessary items from home can be a great way to declutter and generate extra income. With the rise of e-commerce and online marketplaces, entrepreneurs can take advantage of this opportunity by selling items on popular platforms such as Craigslist or Facebook Marketplace. By streamlining the process of selling and purchasing used items, these platforms have made it easier than ever for people to buy and sell items online. This represents a powerful new product or service model that can help to simplify the process of buying and selling goods, while also providing a new source of revenue for many individuals and businesses.

Exercise
- What are some examples of difficult and time-consuming problems that people encounter in their daily lives?
- What are some practical ideas or solutions that can help to address these challenges and make people's lives easier?
- How can entrepreneurs leverage these practical ideas and solutions to develop innovative new product or service models that focus on simplifying everyday life and improving the overall customer experience?

---

[6] Elgendy, Mostafa, Cecilia Sik-Lanyi, and Arpad Kelemen. "Making shopping easy for people with visual impairment using mobile assistive technologies." Applied Sciences 9.6 (2019): 1061.

1.7. Make Products Smarter

Advancements in technology have created opportunities for entrepreneurs to make products and services smarter and more connected.[7] With the introduction of smart locks, for example, it is now possible to remotely control your home's door from your phone, providing added convenience and security. Similarly, a device that detects changes in the humidity level in your home can warn you of potential leaks and allow you to take action before any significant damage occurs. By leveraging the power of technology to create smarter and more intuitive products, entrepreneurs can provide unique value to their customers and create new business opportunities. This represents a significant shift in the way that products are designed and developed, and presents a promising new frontier for innovation and growth in the tech industry.

The potential for smart products goes far beyond just locks and leak sensors. For example, a new type of smart blanket is now available that incorporates sensors to provide a customized and comfortable sleeping experience. This innovative product can adjust its temperature to match the body temperature of the person using it, ensuring that they stay comfortable and cozy throughout the night. By combining the latest sensor technology with cutting-edge design, this type of product provides an unparalleled level of personalization and convenience, and offers a glimpse into the future of smart home and lifestyle products. With the potential to revolutionize a wide range of industries and markets, entrepreneurs who can capitalize on the growing trend towards smart and connected products stand to gain a significant advantage in the marketplace.

Exercise
- What are some examples of traditional products or services that could benefit from a smart upgrade?
- How can entrepreneurs leverage the latest technology to make these products smarter and more intuitive?
- What are some smart product ideas that could revolutionize the way that people interact with everyday items, and provide new value and convenience to customers?

---

[7] Mühlhäuser, Max. "Smart products: An introduction." *Constructing Ambient Intelligence: AmI 2007 Workshops Darmstadt, Germany, November 7-10, 2007 Revised Papers*. Springer Berlin Heidelberg, 2008.

1.8. Combine Different Products

"Eminent figures in the sciences have often reported that their creativity, whether entailing discovery or invention, ultimately entails a combinatorial process or procedure."[8] One strategy for developing innovative new products is to combine different existing products or features and create something entirely new. For example, combining an alarm clock with an espresso machine can result in a convenient and effective tool for waking up in the morning. The sound and aroma of freshly brewed coffee can help to stimulate your senses and start your day on the right foot. Similarly, by combining a stroller and a bicycle, entrepreneurs can create a new type of product that meets the needs of mothers who want to stay active and mobile with their children. Another example is the combination of organic, healthy food with delicious baked goods, providing customers with a low-calorie and guilt-free option for indulging their sweet tooth. By identifying opportunities for product fusion and leveraging the unique characteristics of each, entrepreneurs can create exciting new products that offer real value to consumers.

Exercise
- What are some examples of existing products or services that could be combined to create something new and innovative?
- How can entrepreneurs identify opportunities for product fusion, and develop effective strategies for combining different features and characteristics?
- What are some potential advantages and challenges of creating combination products or services, and how can entrepreneurs mitigate risk and maximize value for their customers?

---

[8] Simonton, Dean Keith. "Scientific creativity: Discovery and invention as combinatorial." *Frontiers in Psychology* 12 (2021): 721104.

1.9. Turn your hobby into a business

Transforming a hobby into a business is a fulfilling way to turn your passion into a profitable venture. Many successful businesses have been built around people's hobbies and interests,[9] such as Steve Jobs' thriving computer company that grew from his hobby in electronics. Similarly, Terry Finley started buying racehorses and selling partial ownership in them to create a company centered around his love for racehorses.

If you have a hobby that you're passionate about, consider exploring whether it could be turned into a business. By leveraging your skills and interests, you can create a unique and fulfilling career that allows you to do what you love and make money at the same time.

For example, if you're passionate about chess, you could produce and sell chess sets, books, and souvenirs for other chess enthusiasts. Offering chess classes, organizing clubs, and holding tournaments are other ways to monetize your hobby.

If you're passionate about baking healthy, low-calorie cookies and cakes, you could start by developing and selling your own line of products. You could also offer your treats at local farmers' markets or health food stores. Opening a café with a bakery that specializes in healthy and low-calorie baked goods is another option.

By turning your love of baking or chess into a business, you can share your passion with others while also earning a living doing something you enjoy. So, if you have a hobby that you're passionate about, consider exploring the ways in which it could be transformed into a profitable venture.

Exercise
- Can you provide some examples of successful businesses that were started by people around you turning their hobbies or interests into a profitable venture?
- Which of your hobbies do you think has the potential to be turned into a profitable business by creating a product or line of products?
- What hobbies do you think could be turned into a profitable business by offering them as a service or set of services?

---

[9] Kadile, Vita, and Alessandro Biraglia. "From hobby to business: Exploring environmental antecedents of entrepreneurial alertness using fsQCA." *Journal of Small Business Management* 60.3 (2022): 580-615.

1.10. Make things and chores more entertaining

"Gamification is the concept that utilizing elements and ideas of video games in non-gaming fields."[10] People are looking for more enjoyable moments through games and playful stuff in their lives. Many people are willing to spend money on products that offer entertainment or novelty value. This is evident in the popularity of items such as robot-shaped vacuum cleaners, which add a touch of humor to the mundane task of cleaning, or bicycle-shaped pizza cutters, which are not only functional but also decorative and entertaining. By adding a touch of fun or playfulness to everyday items or chores, entrepreneurs can create new value for their customers and drive success in their businesses. These types of products have the potential to appeal to a wide range of consumers, particularly those who are looking for ways to make their daily lives more enjoyable and engaging.

Another example of making daily activities more entertaining is the integration of music into the act of brushing teeth. The Arm & Hammer Tooth Tunes Toothbrush, which plays the song "What Makes You Beautiful" while brushing, is a great example of how entrepreneurs can add an element of fun and excitement to mundane activities. By offering a unique and enjoyable experience, this type of product has the potential to capture the attention of consumers and stand out in a crowded market. These types of innovative and entertaining products are not only fun for customers, but they also have the potential to create new business opportunities and drive growth for entrepreneurs who are willing to think outside the box.

Exercise
- What are some examples of boring or mundane tasks or chores that people encounter in their daily lives?
- What are some practical ideas or solutions that can be implemented to make these tasks more engaging or entertaining?
- How can entrepreneurs leverage these ideas to develop new product or service models that incorporate elements of entertainment, novelty, or fun, and create new value for their customers?

---

[10] Kim, Bohyun. "Gamification." *Library Technology Reports* 51.2 (2015): 10-18.

1.11. Sell an experience

To create a successful business, consider offering customers an unforgettable experience. "Customer experiences have been considered to be a key concept in marketing management."[11] Many people are searching for unique and unforgettable experiences to add excitement to their lives after the monotony of their daily routines.

For instance, wine enthusiasts may be interested in the opportunity to work in a vineyard for a week, as this provides a one-of-a-kind experience that they may value more than a traditional vacation at a resort.

An example of selling an experience could be targeting healthy-lifestyle people and offering a day-long farming experience on a real farm. This could include activities such as milking cows and goats, cutting sheep wool, soaking the sow, grooming horses, and collecting eggs.

People who are passionate about healthy living and sustainability might be willing to pay more for this unique and immersive experience than for a typical vacation at a resort. By focusing on selling an experience rather than just a product or service, you can offer something truly special and memorable that people will be willing to invest in.

By focusing on selling experiences that are out of the ordinary, you can create a successful business that offers something truly unique to your customers.

Exercise
- Who might be interested in purchasing a business idea that sells an experience? Who is the target audience?
- What type of business idea could be centered around offering a unique experience to these people?
- How can an experience concept be developed into a profitable business idea for this specific target group?

---

[11] Tynan, Caroline, and Sally McKechnie. "Experience marketing: a review and reassessment." *Journal of marketing management* 25.5-6 (2009): 501-517.

1.12. The finalist business ideas

To choose a business idea, it's important to consider multiple options and then narrow down your list to a few finalists. Once you have your finalists, you can score each idea to determine its likelihood of success.

While it's important to choose a solid business concept, remember that products and strategies can evolve and change over time. Don't wait for the "perfect" idea; instead, choose one that you feel confident in starting with.

Take another look at the business ideas presented in this chapter and write down the three that stand out to you as the most promising and enjoyable to pursue.

Review the business ideas you've worked on throughout this chapter and identify the top three that align with your interests and have the most potential for success. Write them down and use them to guide your future planning and decision-making as you move forward in developing your business.

Exercise
Now list your top three business ideas.
- What is your number one business idea?
- What is your number second business idea?
- What is your number three business idea?

2 The Art of Choosing: Selecting the Right Business Idea for You

If you're not doing some things that are crazy, then you're do-ing the wrong things.
Larry Page
Co-Founder of Google

2.1. Making a Decision

Now that you have three business ideas in mind, it's time to choose one that you will pursue. Consider these key questions to help make your final decision:

Is the business idea something that you are passionate about and excited to work on? Building a successful business takes time and effort, so it's important to choose something that you will enjoy working on in the long term.

How does your business idea differentiate itself from competitors in the market? A unique selling proposition is critical for success, as customers are always looking for something new and better.

Is the business idea scalable? You want to make sure that there is enough demand in the market to support exponential growth, otherwise, it will remain a small business.

What is the cost of initial investment, and what is the potential speed of return on your investment? Understanding the upfront investment costs and the expected return on investment is critical. You want to make sure that you are not putting in more money than you can afford and that the business will generate returns in a reasonable timeframe.

Consider these questions carefully to select the best business idea for you and your goals.

2.2. How do you like the business idea?

Starting a business is a challenging endeavor that requires a significant investment of time and resources, as well as a willingness to take risks. As a startup founder, you are committing yourself to a long-term journey that may not yield immediate returns.

Therefore, it is crucial to ensure that you genuinely like the business idea you are pursuing. While financial promise is essential, your passion for the idea will help you sustain your commitment and motivation in the long run.

In addition, your business idea should align with your sense of purpose, as having a genuine connection to your idea will help you communicate its value and impact to others.

It is also important to consider the potential impact of your business on your family relationships. Ensuring that your loved ones believe in and support your business idea can help minimize conflict and provide an additional source of motivation and encouragement.

In summary, starting a business requires commitment, passion, purpose, and support from loved ones. Consider all of these factors as you evaluate your business ideas and choose the one that aligns best with your values and goals.

Let's consider a case study with three competing business ideas: opening a café and bakery, selling designer clothes online, and selling a simple, colorful notepad app on Appstore and Google Play.

When evaluating these three business ideas, there are several important factors to consider. First, it's important to assess your personal interest and passion for each idea. Which one excites you the most and feels like a natural fit for your skills and interests?

It's important to consider how the idea is different or better and how it can provide a unique value proposition to customers. Being better or different can help a business capture customers' attention and gain an advantage over competitors.

Another important factor to consider is the potential scalability and growth opportunities for each business idea. Can the café and bakery expand to multiple locations or franchise opportunities? Is there potential to expand the designer clothing business into new markets or product lines? Will the notepad app be popular enough to generate significant revenue and be developed into additional products?

Next, it's important to evaluate the market demand for each business idea. How many people are already buying designer clothes online, and how much competition is there in that space? Is there a gap in the market for a simple, easy-to-use notepad app, or are there already many similar options available?

Finally, it's important to consider the financial implications of each business idea. How much initial investment is required, and what is the potential return on investment? Which business idea has the highest potential for generating profits in the short and long term?

By carefully evaluating these factors and weighing the pros and cons of each business idea, you can make an informed decision and choose the one that is most likely to succeed and bring you the greatest satisfaction and financial success.

2.3. Which one do you like most?

When considering business ideas, it's important to reflect on why you like a particular idea. Is it because you have a passion for the industry or the product/service? Or do you see a market opportunity that excites you? Understanding your motivations for liking the idea can help you stay committed to it in the long run.

For example, let's say you have three business ideas: opening a café and bakery, selling designer clothes online, and selling a simple colorful notepad app on Appstore and Google-Play. If you're passionate about baking and creating healthy food, then opening a café and bakery would align with your interests and motivate you to commit to the business idea.

Next, it's important to consider whether the idea resonates with your personal story and sense of mission. This can help you create a genuine and authentic brand that resonates with your customers. For example, if you're passionate about healthy eating, opening a café and bakery that specializes in healthy and organic foods would align with your personal mission and values. Similarly, if you have a background in design, selling designer clothes online could be a good fit for your personal story.

Finally, it's essential to consider whether your loved ones will believe in and support your idea. Starting a business can be a significant undertaking that requires time, effort, and resources. Having the support of your loved ones can make a big difference in your ability to see the idea through to success. For example, if you're selling a notepad app, you may need the support of your partner or family to help spread the word and generate interest in the app.

Example
To evaluate each business idea, ask yourself the following questions and score each idea accordingly:

I like the idea because...
- For the café and bakery idea, I like the idea because I enjoy baking and creating delicious and healthy food, and I think there's a market for it in my local area. Score: 8/10
- For the designer clothes online idea, I like the idea because I have a passion for fashion and I see a market opportunity for selling designer clothes at affordable prices. Score: 7/10
- For the simple notepad app idea, I like the idea because I think there's a need for a user-friendly and visually appealing notepad app on the Appstore and Google Play. Score: 6/10

It resonates with my personal story and my sense of mission because...

- For the café and bakery idea, it resonates with my personal story and mission because I value healthy eating and I want to provide delicious and nutritious options for people in my community. Score: 9/10
- For the designer clothes online idea, it resonates with my personal story and mission because I want to make designer clothes more accessible and affordable for people who share my passion for fashion. Score: 6/10
- For the simple notepad app idea, it resonates with my personal story and mission because I want to simplify people's lives and help them stay organized in a digital age. Score: 7/10

I can make my family believe in my business idea because...
- For the café and bakery idea, I can make my family believe in the idea because I can offer them free samples and get their feedback, as well as involve them in the business planning process. Score: 9/10
- For the designer clothes online idea, I can make my family believe in the idea by showing them the potential market and explaining my passion for fashion and my vision for the business. Score: 7/10
- For the simple notepad app idea, I can make my family believe in the idea by showing them the potential demand for a user-friendly notepad app and explaining how it can simplify people's lives. Score: 8/10

Exercise
Now complete the following sentences for each business idea and provide a score for each idea to compare them.
- I like the idea because
- It resonates with my personal story and my sense of mission because
- I can make my family believe in my business idea because

2.4. Is it different or better?

When evaluating your business ideas, it's crucial to consider their uniqueness and competitiveness in the market. How do they stand out from existing offerings? Are they better, faster, or more cost-effective? Can they solve a problem in a new or more effective way? Understanding the differentiation and competitive advantage of your ideas is essential to their success and growth potential. Take the time to research and analyze the market to determine if your ideas have the potential to stand out and meet the needs of customers in a unique and valuable way.

Evaluate each of your business ideas carefully and objectively. Ask yourself if each idea is truly different and better than what is already available on the market. Give each idea a score based on this evaluation, considering factors such as the unique value proposition, market demand, and competition. Be honest with yourself, and don't hesitate to eliminate ideas that do not score well in this evaluation. Remember, a successful business idea must offer something unique and valuable to customers.

Example
When evaluating your business ideas, it's important to determine how they differ from what's already available on the market. For example, if you're considering opening a café and bakery, you might differentiate yourself by baking healthy, organic, and low-calorie food. On a scale of 1-5, you might score this idea a 5 for its uniqueness and potential to stand out.

Similarly, if you're thinking about selling designer clothes online, you might set yourself apart by choosing unique designs that aren't available in stores. On a scale of 1-5, you might score this idea a 4 for its potential to differentiate from the competition.

On the other hand, if you're planning to sell a simple notepad app on Appstore and Google-Play, the uniqueness of the idea may not be as significant as its ease of use. In this case, you might score the idea a 3 for its simplicity and ease of use, rather than its uniqueness.

In summary, evaluating your business ideas based on how they differ and stand out in the market is an essential step in the planning process. By scoring each idea based on its uniqueness, you can compare and prioritize the ideas to determine which ones have the most potential for success.

Exercise

Now complete the following sentences for each business idea and provide a score for each idea to compare them.

- It is different because
- It is better because

2.5. Is it scalable?

There is broad consensus that a scalable business model plays a key role in new venture success.[12] Scalability is a critical factor to consider when evaluating a business idea's potential success. In essence, scalability refers to the ability of a business to grow and expand its output without significantly increasing its costs. It is a key component of a startup, as startups aim to generate exponential growth in a relatively short time.

The distinction between scalability and non-scalability often comes down to the relationship between costs and revenue. Traditional small businesses have a sales-cost growth relationship. When sales increase, costs also rise, limiting growth potential. This relationship is why small businesses often struggle to achieve significant growth without experiencing a corresponding increase in costs.

Scalable businesses, on the other hand, can generate revenue growth while keeping costs stable or increasing them at a slower rate. For example, a software company can sell more copies of its product without needing to produce more physical copies or hire more employees. This means that profits can grow exponentially without increasing expenses.

The key to scalability is finding ways to generate value without incurring significant additional costs. This can involve focusing on products or services that have low variable costs and high demand, such as software or digital products. Other scalable business models include franchising, subscription-based models, and other forms of recurring revenue.

However, it's important to note that scalability is not a one-size-fits-all solution. Some business models simply are not scalable due to the inherent nature of their products or services. For example, a restaurant cannot significantly grow without increasing the number of customers served, which means more food, supplies, and employees. Similarly, a tailoring business would need to hire more skilled workers to open new locations and meet growing demand.

In conclusion, scalability is a vital factor in evaluating a business idea's potential success. It is about creating a business model that can achieve exponential growth without a corresponding increase in costs. Scalability is an essential characteristic of successful startups, and understanding it can help entrepreneurs create more effective and sustainable businesses.

---

[12] Stampfl, Georg, Reinhard Prügl, and Vincent Osterloh. "An explorative model of business model scalability." *International Journal of Product Development* 18.3-4 (2013): 226-248.

Example
When evaluating the scalability of a business idea, it is important to consider a few key factors. Firstly, it is important to understand if the business output requires increased input in order to grow. For example, with the business idea of opening a café and bakery, investment would be needed for each new shop in order to expand the business. This results in a low score of 1. Similarly, selling designer clothes online would require buying more goods for each new dress, resulting in a low score of 1 as well. However, a simple notepad app on the App Store and Google Play can be easily downloaded, making it highly scalable with a score of 5.

The core service or product of the business is another factor to consider in scalability. In the case of opening a café and bakery, baking with recipes and franchising with an operational book can be easily duplicated, resulting in a score of 4. However, designer clothes are unique and hard to find, which makes it difficult to duplicate and score lower at 2. Conversely, the simple notepad app can be easily duplicated, making it highly scalable with a score of 5.

Lastly, it is important to consider if there is a big or growing demand for the product or service. In the case of the café and bakery, bakery products are popular all around the world, which results in a high score of 5. Selling designer clothes online may not have a big market since they are not for mass consumption, resulting in a low score of 2. However, the simple notepad app has a broad market since everyone who has a phone uses a note-taking app, resulting in a high score of 5.

Overall, when evaluating the scalability of a business idea, it is important to consider whether the business output requires increased input to grow, if the core service or product is easy to duplicate for each customer, and if there is a big or growing demand for the product or service. By analyzing these factors, we can better understand the scalability of a business idea and its potential for success.

Exercise
Provide a score for each business idea to compare them.
- Is an increase in input necessary for business output to grow?
- Can the core service or product be easily replicated for each customer?
- Is there a high demand or a growing demand for the product or service?

2.6. Is there a market demand?

Market demand is not necessarily the sole, or even the principal, determinant of the scale and direction of inventive and innovative activity.[13] Understanding the market demand is crucial for any business idea. It's important to evaluate the market size, competition, and potential growth.

If the market demand for a particular product or service is low or shrinking, it becomes increasingly difficult for a business to survive and grow. Low demand means that there are fewer customers interested in buying the product or service, which results in lower sales and revenue. This can lead to the business operating at a loss, and in severe cases, it may result in the business shutting down.

Shrinking demand can also have a similar effect. If the market for a particular product or service is getting smaller over time, it means that there is less demand for it. This could be due to changes in consumer behavior or preferences, technological advances, or economic factors. As a result, the business may need to adapt or pivot to stay relevant, or risk becoming obsolete.

When considering selling designer clothes online, for example, it's important to assess the existing market size and competition. How many people are already buying designer clothes online, and how many similar businesses are out there? This information will give an idea of the market saturation and the potential for growth.

On the other hand, if the business idea is to sell a simple notepad app on the app store, it's important to assess whether there's a gap in the market for such an app. Are there already many similar options available, or does the proposed app offer something unique that differentiates it from the competition? Assessing the market demand and competition is essential for identifying the potential for growth and success of the business idea.

Moreover, the market demand should be growing or have the potential for growth. In the case of the notepad app, if the demand is not growing or the market is already saturated, there may be limited potential for success. However, if the market is growing, and there's a demand for an easy-to-use notepad app, then the business idea may have a higher potential for success. Therefore, it's important to assess the market demand and growth potential to determine the viability of the business idea.

---

[13] Freeman, Christopher. "The determinants of innovation: Market demand, technology, and the response to social problems." *Futures* 11.3 (1979): 206-215.

Exercise
Provide a score for each business idea to compare them.

- What is the size of the potential market for this product or service?
- Are there any existing market trends that suggest a growing or shrinking demand for this type of product or service?
- Is there an unfulfilled need or gap in the market that this product or service can address?

2.7. What are the financial implications?

A common cause of small business failures at different stages of the business's life cycle is often attributed to inadequate financial planning, which can lead to cash flow challenges and unsustainable operations. By neglecting to establish sound financial strategies, businesses may struggle to effectively manage their resources and navigate potential pitfalls, ultimately jeopardizing their long-term viability.[14]

When evaluating potential business ideas, it's important to consider the financial implications of each one. This means taking a close look at the potential costs, revenue, and profit margins associated with each idea. By understanding the financial implications of each option, you can make a more informed decision about which idea to pursue.

One of the most important things to consider is the initial investment required to get each business idea off the ground. Some business ideas may require significant upfront costs, such as buying or leasing a property, purchasing equipment, or hiring employees. Other ideas may have lower startup costs, but may require ongoing expenses like inventory, marketing, or insurance. By carefully evaluating the financial requirements of each idea, you can get a better sense of which ones are feasible given your budget and resources.

Another important financial consideration is the potential revenue that each idea can generate. This means estimating the sales that each business idea can generate and projecting the potential profit margins. You may also need to consider factors like pricing, competition, and market demand. Understanding the revenue potential of each idea is essential for making informed decisions about which one to pursue.

In addition to these factors, it's also important to consider the ongoing costs and risks associated with each idea. Some business ideas may be more expensive to maintain over time, or may carry greater risks due to factors like ma
rket volatility or regulatory changes. By evaluating the long-term financial implications of each idea, you can better assess the potential risks and rewards.

---

[14] Davila, Antonio, and George Foster. "Management control systems in early-stage startup companies." *The accounting review* 82.4 (2007): 907-937.

Overall, understanding the financial implications of each business idea is essential for making informed decisions about which one to pursue. By carefully evaluating the costs, revenue potential, and ongoing risks and challenges associated with each option, you can choose the idea that offers the best chance of success while also aligning with your goals and resources.

Example

Opening a café and bakery may require significant investment in equipment, personnel, and space rental. The potential return on investment may vary depending on the location, market competition, and the quality of the products. In comparison, selling designer clothes online may require less initial investment, but the competition is likely to be high, and the profit margins may be lower. On the other hand, selling a simple colorful notepad app on the Appstore and Google-Play may require less initial investment, and the potential profit margin may be higher, especially if the app gains traction and popularity. However, there is still the risk that the market may become saturated with similar apps or that demand may decrease over time.

Understanding the financial implications of each business idea is crucial to making an informed decision. It helps to determine the level of investment needed, the potential return on investment, and the long-term profitability of the business. By asking questions the below, a potential business owner can weigh the pros and cons of each option and choose the one that offers the highest potential for success.

Exercise

Provide a score for each business idea to compare them.
- How much initial investment is required, and
- What is the potential return on investment?
- Which business idea has the highest potential for generating profits in the short and long term?

2.8. The Finalist Business Idea

Exercise

In this exercise, calculate the total scores for each business idea by adding up the scores from previous evaluations. This will help you to compare the overall potential of each idea and make an informed decision about which one is most promising for your business.

By comparing the total scores, you can gain a more comprehensive understanding of each idea's strengths and weaknesses, as well as their overall potential for generating profits. This information can be invaluable in making an informed decision about which business idea to pursue.

In addition, by taking a structured approach to evaluating and comparing business ideas, you can minimize the risk of making a decision based solely on intuition or personal bias. Instead, you can make a data-driven decision that is more likely to lead to success in the long run.

2.9. Comparison Table

**Use the scores from previous tables
(1 is lowest and 5 is highest score)**

Business Idea Description	Idea A	Idea B	Idea C
Which one do you like most?			
Is it different or better?			
Is it scalable?			
Is the cost of investment low?			
Total Scores			
The Finalist Idea			

3 Customer Solutions: How to Identify and Solve Problems for Your Market

"Every once in a while, a new technology, an old problem, and a big idea turn in-to an innovation. "
Dean Kamen
Inventor of Segway

3.1. Think About Customer Problems

After selecting a business idea in the previous chapter, it's time to shift your focus to identifying the problem your business idea will solve. Instead of simply offering a product, your business should provide a solution to customers' needs.

In this chapter, you'll define a problem or a gap in the market that your business idea can address. You'll dive deep into the challenges customers are experiencing and present your solution to these issues.

To do this, you'll create a problem and solution scenario that forms the basis of your company's product or service. You'll need to provide a detailed description of the problem and the benefits of your solution. This will help you to effectively communicate your value proposition to potential customers and investors.

3.2. The Aim and Need

Customers seek products that fulfill a specific need or accomplish a desired outcome. They are not solely interested in purchasing a product for its own sake but rather for the value it can provide in solving their problems or achieving their goals. This customer-centric perspective, as emphasized by Theodore Levitt, highlights the importance of understanding the underlying purpose or result that customers are seeking. By focusing on delivering solutions and satisfying customer needs, entrepreneurs can better align their products or services with the desired outcomes, enhancing customer satisfaction and driving business success.[15]

The difference between a customer's aim and need lies in their underlying motivations and desires. While both terms are related to a customer's requirements, they address different aspects of their decision-making process.

A customer's need refers to a specific problem or requirement that they have, which prompts them to seek a solution. It represents the functional or practical aspect of their request. For example, a customer may need a new laptop because their current one is slow and outdated, hindering their work efficiency. In this case, the need is driven by a practical necessity to improve performance and productivity.

On the other hand, a customer's aim refers to their broader objectives, aspirations, or desired outcomes that extend beyond the basic need. It encapsulates the emotional, psychological, or aspirational aspects of their request. A customer's aim is often tied to their personal preferences, values, or goals. Using the previous example, the customer's aim might be to have a high-performance laptop that enables them to pursue their passion for graphic design or video editing, allowing them to express their creativity and achieve professional recognition.

While needs are essential for identifying the core requirements, aims provide additional context and insights into a customer's desires and motivations. Understanding both the needs and aims of customers is crucial for businesses to effectively cater to their requirements and provide a satisfactory experience.

---

[15] Christensen, Clayton M., Scott Cook, and Taddy Hall. "What customers want from your products." *Harvard Business School Newsletter: Working Knowledge* (2006).

By recognizing and addressing a customer's needs, a business can offer functional solutions that meet their specific requirements. However, by understanding a customer's aims, a business can go beyond meeting the basic need and provide additional value by aligning their products or services with the customer's aspirations, preferences, or emotional satisfaction. This approach allows businesses to build stronger connections with customers, differentiate themselves from competitors, and create more meaningful and long-lasting relationships.

To summarize, a customer's need represents the practical requirements that drive their demand for a particular product or service, while a customer's aim encompasses their broader objectives, aspirations, or desired outcomes. Both factors play a crucial role in understanding and satisfying customer expectations, allowing businesses to deliver personalized and meaningful solutions.

Exercise:
- What is the customer's aim or objective in the field for which you intend to offer products or services? What is the specific outcome or goal that the customer is striving to accomplish?

- What is the customer's need or requirement in the field where you want to provide products or services? What are the specific challenges or demands that the customer is seeking to address?

3.3. The Incident/Problem

Incidents and problems are distinct concepts. An incident refers to a disruption or interruption in a service, while a problem represents the underlying cause of that interruption.[16] For instance, when a computer software crashes, it is considered an incident, and the problem lies within the coding. Incidents are visible on the surface, while problems reside beneath them.

Example
- What is the specific incident that the customer is currently experiencing?
- The customer is experiencing confusion and desires to take a note, but they are unsure how to proceed.
- What is the underlying cause of the problem that leads to the incident or complaint?
- Regarding the confusion and difficulty in note-taking, the problem might stem from the notepad app that has an excessive number of features, making the process complex and time-consuming.

Exercise
- What is the specific incident that the customer is currently experiencing?
- What is the underlying cause of the problem that leads to the incident or complaint?

---

[16] Kapella, Victor. "A framework for incident and problem management." *International Network Services whitepaper* (2003).

3.4. Solution

The importance of finding a solution that satisfies customers cannot be understated. When customers encounter problems or challenges, having an effective solution is crucial to their overall satisfaction and experience. By offering a suitable solution, customers can overcome their issues and achieve the desired outcome, leading to a sense of contentment and fulfillment. For instance, let's consider a scenario where a customer is facing the problem of chronic back pain due to an uncomfortable mattress. In this case, our solution could involve providing a specialized orthopedic mattress designed to alleviate pressure points and provide optimal spinal alignment. The customer, upon using the new mattress, would experience improved comfort and reduced back pain, leading to a significant increase in satisfaction and overall well-being. This scenario exemplifies the significance of offering tailored solutions that directly address customers' problems, as it can profoundly impact their lives and contribute to their overall happiness and contentment.

In the realm of new business development, the concept of customer scenarios is often overlooked by many companies. The customer scenario refers to the broader context in which customers make decisions, purchase products, and utilize services. Neglecting to understand and address these scenarios can result in missed opportunities to cultivate customer loyalty and drive sales growth, as highlighted by consultant Patricia Seybold.[17]

Example:
What solution do you propose to address the customer's needs? How will the customer experience satisfaction as a result of your solution? Can you provide a scenario example of a customer's problem and how your solution resolves it?

A woman begins her weekday by wearing low heel shoes (Number 1) as she commutes on the subway, enjoying a comfortable standing experience. Upon arriving at her office, she switches to high heels (Number 5). After a busy workday, just before leaving to meet her husband for dinner, she transitions to mid-height heels (Number 3). When she returns home, she can peacefully sleep without any foot pain. This new product eliminates the need for her to carry multiple pairs of shoes for different occasions, providing convenience and comfort throughout her day.

---

[17] Seybold, Patricia B. "Get inside the lives of your customers." *Harvard Business Review* 79.5 (2001): 80-9.

Exercise

What solution do you propose to address the customer's needs? How will the customer experience satisfaction as a result of your solution? Can you provide a scenario example of a customer's problem and how your solution resolves it?

Solution:

Scenario:

3.5. Solution Map

Creating a visual solution map can be an effective way to illustrate and communicate the proposed solution in a clear and engaging manner. Visual elements such as graphics, pictures, and flowcharts can help convey complex ideas, processes, or scenarios in a more accessible format. By visually representing the solution, it becomes easier for the audience to understand the concept, visualize the steps involved, and grasp the benefits it offers.

The sequence of activities that customers engage to solve a problem is called a customer activity cycle.[18]

Example: Notepad App

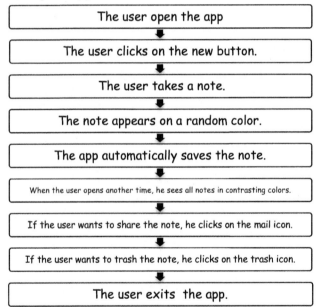

The user open the app
↓
The user clicks on the new button.
↓
The user takes a note.
↓
The note appears on a random color.
↓
The app automatically saves the note.
↓
When the user opens another time, he sees all notes in contrasting colors.
↓
If the user wants to share the note, he clicks on the mail icon.
↓
If the user wants to trash the note, he clicks on the trash icon.
↓
The user exits the app.

Exercise
Enhance your solution presentation with visuals like graphics, pictures, or flowcharts. Consider creating a video that explains the scenario, showcasing the benefits of your proposed solution.

---

[18] Dontchev, Asen L., R. Tyrrell Rockafellar, and R. Tyrrell Rockafellar. *Implicit functions and solution mappings: A view from variational analysis*. Vol. 11. New York: Springer, 2009.

3.6. Features and Benefits of Your Product

When evaluating a product or service, it's important to understand both its features and benefits. Features refer to the specific characteristics or qualities that the product or service possesses. These can include functionalities, specifications, or components that make it unique. For example, a smartphone may have features such as a large display, a powerful processor, and multiple camera lenses.

On the other hand, benefits are the advantages or positive outcomes that customers gain from using the product or service.[19] They address the needs or desires of customers and provide solutions or fulfillments. In the case of the smartphone, the benefits could be a visually immersive experience, fast and efficient performance, and high-quality photos. Understanding both the features and benefits allows customers to make informed decisions by assessing how the product or service aligns with their requirements and how it can positively impact their lives.

Exercise
- What are the features of your product or services?
- What are the benefits of your product or services?

---

[19] Crosling, M. (2023, February 14). *Know the Difference Between Features and Benefits.* Retrieved June 8, 2023, from https://strategiccontent.co/difference-between-features-and-benefits/

3.7. Barriers to Entry

Barriers to entry are obstacles or challenges that make it difficult for new competitors to enter a specific industry or market.[20] These barriers can arise from various factors, including financial, legal, technological, or strategic considerations. Financial barriers often stem from the high initial investment required to establish operations, develop infrastructure, or build brand recognition. Legal barriers may involve regulatory requirements, licenses, or patents that limit entry to certain players. Technological barriers may arise from the need for specialized knowledge or access to advanced technology. Additionally, strategic barriers can emerge from existing dominant players who have established strong customer loyalty, extensive distribution networks, or economies of scale. Overall, barriers to entry serve to protect established firms and can make it challenging for new entrants to compete effectively.

Exercise
- Government Regulation: Are there significant hurdles to obtaining government approval for a particular business or product?
- Startup Costs: What are the financial implications of starting a business in your industry?
- Technology: Is your technology unique or protected by patents?
- Economies of Scale: Does the business model require large-scale production to be financially viable?
- Product Differentiation: How does your product differentiate itself from competing products?
- Access to Suppliers and Distribution Channels: Are there barriers for firms to access suppliers and distribute their products in the market?

---

[20] Pehrsson, Anders. "Barriers to entry and market strategy: a literature review and a proposed model." *European Business Review* 21.1 (2009): 64-77.

4 The Power of Proposition: Building a Business Model with Value

"Your customers are the judge, jury, and executioner of your value proposition. They will be merciless if you don't find fit!"
Alexander Osterwalder,
Value Proposition Design: How to Create Products and Services Customers Want

4.1. What is your value proposition?

Value proposition refers to a concise business or marketing statement employed by a company to convey why a consumer should choose their product or service.[21] This statement is designed to persuade potential customers that the specific offering will provide greater value or offer a superior solution to a problem compared to similar alternatives in the market. The value proposition encapsulates the unique benefits, advantages, or distinctive features of the product or service, showcasing its value proposition in a compelling and persuasive manner. It aims to differentiate the offering from competitors and convince consumers that choosing it will result in a more favorable outcome or experience. The value proposition serves as a powerful tool to communicate the core value and appeal of a product or service, ultimately influencing the purchasing decisions of consumers.

Example
Uber's Value Proposition:
- With just a tap, a car arrives at your location promptly.
- Your driver has precise knowledge of your destination, ensuring a smooth journey.
- Payment is seamlessly processed through a cashless system.

Simple Notepad's Value Proposition:
- Simple yet distinctive note-taking experience that is user-friendly.

Exercise
What is your value proposition? Explain your value proposition for the customer in a succinct and understandable way.

---

[21] Osterwalder, Alexander, et al. *Value proposition design: How to create products and services customers want.* John Wiley & Sons, 2015.

4.2. Business Model

A business model refers to a company's strategic plan for generating revenue and achieving profitability.[22] It outlines the products or services the business will produce and market, as well as the methods it will employ to do so. Additionally, a business model encompasses the expenses that will be incurred in the process. Various types of business models exist, including direct sales, franchising, advertising-based models, and brick-and-mortar establishments. Furthermore, there are click-and-mortar models that combine physical and online presence. It is essential for a business model to consider both sources of income and significant expenses to create value effectively.

Exercise
Define your sources of income in your business model.

Incomes
- Sales of product and services
- Rent income
- Advertising
- Royalties
- Licensing fee
- Interest income
.....
.....
.....

Expenses.
Define your expenses. Having a clear understanding of expenses is crucial for a comprehensive business model. Without accurately predicting the major costs, income projections become ineffective and meaningless.
- Rent
- Salaries
- Equipment
- Material costs
- Marketing and Advertising costs
- Official licensing costs
- Loan payments
.....
.....
.....

---

[22] Osterwalder, Alexander, et al. "Business model generation." *Business Model* (2005).

5 Stand Out: Positioning Your Business in a Competitive Market

"The basic approach of positioning is not to create something new and different, but to
manipulate what's
already up there in the mind, to retie the connections that already exist."
Al Reis,
Positioning:
The Battle for Your Mind: How to be Seen and Heard in the Overcrowded Marketplace

5.1. The Market

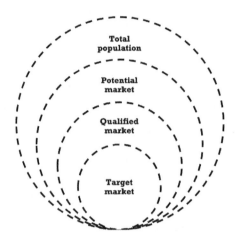

The Total Population refers to the entire population of a specific market, such as a city, state, country, or continent. It represents the entire pool of individuals within that geographic region.

The Potential Market, on the other hand, consists of those individuals within the total population who have an expressed interest or need to acquire a particular product or service. This group represents the segment of the population that shows potential demand.[23]

The Qualified Market narrows down the potential market further by focusing on individuals who not only have the interest in the product or service but also possess the financial means and capability to make a purchase. For example, while many people may desire a luxury sports car, the qualified market would consist of those who have both the financial resources and a valid driver's license.

The Target Market refers to a specific group of consumers that a company aims to sell its products and services to. This group is often defined by factors such as geographic location, buying power, demographics (such as age, gender, income), and psychographics (such as interests, values, lifestyles). By targeting a specific market segment, companies can tailor their marketing strategies and offerings to better meet the needs and preferences of that particular group, increasing the chances of success.

[23] Market Definition, Conceptual Diagram, NetMBA, http://www.netmba.com/marketing/market/definition, retrieved on June 8, 2023.

5.2. The Target Market

A market encompasses all the buyers and sellers within a specific area or region, which can range from a particular group of internet users to cities, regions, states, or countries.

When analyzing a market, it is important to consider the prevailing trends that shape it. Is the market growing, stable, or shrinking? Investing in a growing market offers more opportunities for growth, while a stable and mature market requires competitiveness to gain a market share. It is advisable to avoid investing in a shrinking market as it is likely to decline in the future.

However, it is essential to narrow down your focus from the general market to a specific target market. The term "target" implies the need to refine your market scope. A target market is a group of people that have been identified as the most likely potential customers for a product because of their shared characteristics, such as age, income, and lifestyle.[24] Starting with the total population, you must progressively narrow your market segment to reach your target market.

On the other hand, understanding the existence of a broader market provides opportunities to evaluate different possibilities. In the future, you may consider shifting your target market within the larger market based on changing circumstances or business objectives.

[24] Margaret James, What Is a Target Market?, https://www.investopedia.com/terms/t/target-market.asp, retrieved on June 8, 2023.

5.3. Market Trends

Markets are influenced by three types of trends: Short-Term Trends, Intermediate-Term Trends, and Long-Term Trends. By focusing on long-term trends, a startup can gain insights to anticipate future developments and plan accordingly.

Several trends shape industries, including Technology Trends, Consumption Trends, Demographic Trends, Political Trends, Legal Trends, Economic Trends, and Business Market Trends. Each of these trends has the potential to impact market growth, either by expanding or contracting the market size. Considering these trends becomes vital prior to starting a business, as it allows for informed decision-making and a better understanding of the market landscape.

Short-Term Trends: These are trends that have a relatively brief impact on the market, such as seasonal fluctuations in consumer demand (e.g., increased demand for swimsuits during the summer season).
Intermediate-Term Trends: These trends span a longer duration and can have significant effects on the market, like evolving customer preferences for healthier food options (e.g., the increasing demand for plant-based *alternatives).*

Long-Term Trends: These trends have a lasting impact on the market, often transforming industries over time, such as the shift towards renewable energy sources due to growing environmental concerns (e.g., the increasing adoption of solar power).

Technology Trends: These trends involve advancements in technology that shape markets, such as the rise of artificial intelligence (AI) and its impact on various industries (e.g., AI-powered chatbots transforming customer service interactions).

Consumption Trends: These trends reflect changing consumer behaviors and preferences, like the increasing preference for online shopping and e-commerce platforms (e.g., the growth of online retail giants like Amazon).
Demographic Trends: These trends pertain to shifts in population characteristics, such as the aging population and its impact on healthcare and senior care services (e.g., increased demand for specialized elderly care facilities).

Political Trends: These trends encompass changes in governmental policies or regulations that influence market conditions, such as trade agreements affecting international business operations (e.g., the impact of Brexit on trade relationships between the UK and EU).

Legal Trends: These trends involve changes in laws and regulations that can affect market dynamics, such as data privacy regulations like the

General Data Protection Regulation (GDPR) impacting the digital marketing industry.

Economic Trends: These trends refer to the overall state of the economy and its impact on market conditions, such as economic recessions affecting consumer spending patterns and business investments.

Business Market Trends: These trends focus on specific factors within the business environment, such as increasing competition in a particular industry due to new market entrants or disruptive innovations (e.g., the rise of ride-sharing companies challenging the traditional taxi industry).

Exercise

Identify and analyze the trends that are currently shaping your market by considering the following:

Trend Area:

- Technology Trends
- Consumption Trends
- Demographic Trends
- Political Trends
- Legal Trends
- Economic Trends
- Business Market Trends

Prediction:

For each trend area, make a prediction or observation about the direction in which the trend is heading.

Impact on your Business:

Describe how each trend, based on your prediction, may impact your business in terms of opportunities, challenges, or changes in customer behavior or market dynamics.

5.4. Market Segmentation

Market segmentation refers to the practice of dividing a potential customer market into distinct groups or segments based on various characteristics.[25] These segments are formed by grouping consumers who are likely to respond similarly to marketing strategies and share common traits such as interests, needs, or locations.

There are several bases of segmentation that businesses can utilize to define their target market:

1. Demographic: Segmentation based on demographic factors such as age, gender, income, education, occupation, and family size.
2. Geographic: Segmentation based on geographic factors such as location, region, climate, population density, or urban/rural areas.
3. Psychographic: Segmentation based on psychological and lifestyle factors, including personality traits, values, attitudes, interests, and opinions.
4. Behavioral: Segmentation based on consumer behavior, including purchasing patterns, usage habits, brand loyalty, benefits sought, or response to marketing stimuli.
5. Distribution: Segmentation based on how consumers access and purchase products, considering factors such as online vs. offline channels, direct vs. indirect distribution, or retail vs. wholesale.

By employing market segmentation, businesses can effectively identify and target specific customer groups that are more likely to respond positively to their marketing efforts. This approach allows for tailored and personalized marketing strategies that cater to the unique needs and preferences of different consumer segments, ultimately maximizing the effectiveness of marketing campaigns and enhancing customer satisfaction.

---

[25] Frederick, Howard, Donald Kuratko, and Allan O'Connor. Entrepreneurship: Theory/Process/Practice. 4th ed., Cengage Learning, 2016, p. 54.

Exercise

Assuming you have chosen a specific product or service for your business, let's focus on market segmentation. Utilize the following segmentation bases to develop a segmentation strategy for your target market:

1. Demographic Segmentation: Identify three key demographic variables that are relevant to your product or service. Describe how each variable can help in segmenting your target market based on age, gender, income, education, occupation, or other relevant demographic factors.

2. Geographic Segmentation: Consider the geographic variables that can impact your target market. Identify at least three geographic factors such as location, region, climate, or population density that can influence consumer preferences and behavior. Explain how each variable can contribute to segmenting your target market effectively.

3. Psychographic Segmentation: Explore the psychographic characteristics of your target market. Identify three psychographic variables such as personality traits, values, attitudes, interests, or lifestyles that are relevant to your product or service. Describe how these variables can help in segmenting your target market based on their unique psychographic profiles.

4. Behavioral Segmentation: Analyze consumer behavior related to your product or service. Identify three behavioral variables such as purchasing patterns, product usage, brand loyalty, or response to marketing stimuli that can be used for market segmentation. Explain how understanding and segmenting your target market based on these behavioral variables can enhance your marketing efforts.

5. Distribution Segmentation: Consider the distribution preferences of your target market. Identify three distribution variables such as online vs. offline channels, direct vs. indirect distribution, or retail vs. wholesale that can impact consumer accessibility to your product or service. Discuss how these variables can be used for market segmentation and how they can shape your distribution strategy.

By completing this exercise, you will have a comprehensive segmentation strategy based on demographic, geographic, psychographic, behavioral, and distribution variables, allowing you to effectively target and reach your desired customer segments.

5.5. Positioning

Positioning refers to the strategic space that a brand establishes and maintains in the minds of customers, relative to competitors' products.[26] It is the association between a brand and a specific word or concept that customers identify with. For instance, Volvo has positioned itself as a brand synonymous with safety, appealing to customers who prioritize safe driving. Whole Foods has successfully positioned itself as the go-to choice for organic and healthy food. Similarly, Microsoft initially identified itself with operating systems and later with office programs. When a brand successfully occupies a distinct position in the consumer's mind, it establishes a strong connection and makes sales more automatic. Effective branding and positioning are essential for becoming a leader in the minds of potential customers, and it is a continuous journey for companies to maintain their position in the market.

Examples:
Mercedes - Mercedes positions itself as a luxury brand, emphasizing high-quality and premium features in their vehicles.

Chipotle - Chipotle positions itself as a provider of quality Mexican food with integrity, focusing on fresh ingredients, customization, and sustainability.

Dollar Shave Club - Dollar Shave Club positions itself as a low-cost shaving solution with a humorous and disruptive approach, challenging the traditional razor market.

Gillette - Gillette positions itself as the world's best shaving brand, emphasizing superior performance, precision, and advanced technology in their shaving products.

Apple - Apple positions itself as a company that brings about revolutionary changes in the world, focusing on innovation, sleek design, and user-friendly technology across their range of products.

---

[26] Ries, Al, and Jack Trout. Positioning: The Battle for Your Mind. 20th anniversary ed., McGraw-Hill, 2001.

Exercise
Utilize the 5-step template to create your positioning strategy:

Step 1: Define the Target Segment
Identify and define your primary group of customers that you want to target and focus on in your positioning strategy.

Step 2: Find Differentiation Point
Describe what sets your brand or offering apart from your competitors. Identify the unique aspects or attributes that make you stand out in the market.

Step 3: Provide the Proof
List the reasons or evidence that support your positioning claim. Highlight specific features, benefits, or accomplishments that validate your unique value proposition.

Step 4: Craft the Positioning Statement
Write a concise and compelling sentence that clearly explains the value and benefits you are offering to your target segment. It should capture the essence of your brand's positioning.

Step 5: Create a Positioning Slogan
Develop a simple, short, and catchy slogan that encapsulates your positioning statement. It should be memorable and resonate with your target audience.

By following these steps, you can craft an effective positioning strategy that distinguishes your brand and communicates its value proposition to your target segment.

5.6. Final Customer & Positioning Decisions

Now that you have already identified your ideal customer and worked on your preferred positioning strategy, let's articulate and refine it one final time. Answer the following questions to help articulate your positioning strategy with clarity:

Who is your ideal customer?
Revisit and clearly define your target customer segment, considering their demographics, psychographics, behaviors, or any other relevant characteristics.

What is your preferred positioning strategy?
Reiterate and refine your positioning strategy, emphasizing how you want your brand to be perceived in the market and how you differentiate yourself from competitors. Consider factors such as pricing, quality, innovation, customer service, or any unique selling propositions you plan to leverage.

6 Starting Small: The Minimum Viable Product Approach

"If you're not embarrassed by the first version of your product, you've launched too late."

Reid Hoffman, Founder of LinkedIn.

6.1. What is it: Minimum Viable Product

A Minimum Viable Product (MVP) is a prototype that incorporates minimal features necessary to gather feedback from potential customers. This feedback serves as an indicator to proceed or reconsider making a larger investment. Instead of directly investing in product development and manufacturing, startups can mitigate the risk of market rejection by testing their product idea early on using an MVP approach. This allows for early market validation and reduces the risk of wasting resources on a product that may not resonate with customers.

Paper Cup   *Glass Cup*
MVP   *Product*

To better grasp the concept of a Minimum Viable Product (MVP), let's consider a visual example. Suppose you have a groundbreaking idea for a glass cup. Instead of immediately launching into full-scale production, you create a simple paper cup prototype and gather feedback from potential customers about their interest and willingness to invest in such a cup. Based on the data collected, you can then proceed with refining the design of the glass cup.

By employing an MVP approach, you validate the market demand and gather valuable insights before committing to costly manufacturing processes. This iterative method allows for informed decision-making and reduces the risk of investing in a product that may not align with customer preferences or expectations.

It's worth noting that the term "Minimum Viable Product" was coined and defined by Frank Robinson[27] around 2001, and later popularized by Eric Ries[28], becoming a key concept in lean startup methodology.

---

[27] Frank Robinson, A Proven Methodology to Maximize Return on Risk, 2001, http://www.syncdev.com/minimum-viable-product/.

[28] Eric Ries, The Lean Startup, Currency, 2011.

6.2. Benefits to MVP

Benefits Pyramid

The Benefits Pyramid[29] illustrates the three types of benefits associated with the Minimum Viable Product (MVP) concept:

Must-have benefits:
These benefits are derived from the essential features of the product that are expected by customers. Most competing products in the market are likely to provide these features, and they are considered a baseline requirement.

Performance benefits:
Performance benefits refer to the advantages that make a product competitive and satisfactory to customers. These benefits go beyond the basic requirements and provide added value, giving the product an edge over its competitors.

Delighter benefits:
Delighter benefits are the pinnacle of the Benefits Pyramid. They are the features or experiences that exceed customer expectations and create a sense of delight or surprise. Delighter benefits can set a product apart from the competition and generate strong customer loyalty and advocacy.

By understanding and incorporating these three types of benefits into the MVP, businesses can effectively prioritize their development efforts and create a product that not only meets customer expectations but also surpasses them, fostering customer satisfaction and loyalty.

---

[29] Adapted from Dan Olsen's *The Lean Product Playbook: How to Innovate with Minimum Viable Products and Rapid Customer Feedback, 2015, pg. 90.*

6.3. Defining your MVP Benefits and Features

Exercise

To define the features and benefits of your Minimum Viable Product (MVP) from the customer's perspective, consider the following categories and their associated benefits:

Essential Function:

What are the key features that are essential for customers to be able to use the product effectively? Identify the functionalities that address the primary needs and requirements of the target customers.

Performance and Usability:

Which features prioritize performance and usability? Consider functionalities that are easy to use and deliver a smooth and efficient user experience. How do these features enhance the product's overall performance and usability, ensuring customer satisfaction and ease of adoption?

Delightful Features:

What unexpected features can be added to make the customer's experience more enjoyable? Identify functionalities that can add an element of surprise or delight, enhancing customer satisfaction and creating a positive impression of the product.

For each category, describe the specific benefits that customers will experience as a result of these features. Explain how these benefits align with the category and contribute to the overall value proposition of the MVP.

6.4. Testing your product concept by MVP

	Qualitative Tests	Quantitative Tests
Marketing Tests	Marketing materials	Landing page Explainer video Ad campaigns A/B tests Crowdfunding
Product Tests	Hand Sketch Wireframes Mockups Prototypes	Fake door Product analytics

Testing your product concept by MVP [30]

---

[30] Adapted from Dan Olsen's *The Lean Product Playbook: How to Innovate with Minimum Viable Products and Rapid Customer Feedback, 2015, pg. 93.*

6.5. Marketing Material Tests

Marketing materials encompass a wide range of elements that are crucial for promoting a product or service. These materials include, but are not limited to, a web page, a product video, advertisements, emails, brochures, and more.

Webpage - A web page is a contains multiple sections, menus, and links, providing a comprehensive overview of a company, its products or services, and various information relevant to the website's overall theme or purpose. Webpages are designed to provide visitors with a holistic experience, allowing them to explore different sections, navigate through various content, and access additional pages within the website.

Product Video - A product video is a broader term that encompasses videos showcasing the product in action, highlighting its features, demonstrating its functionality, and providing a more detailed view of its use cases. Product videos often showcase the product's design, performance, and user experience, offering a more immersive and visual representation of the product. These videos can be used for marketing, sales, or educational purposes, giving customers a deeper understanding of the product and its benefits.

Advertisements on the web are quite measurable, and they are useful to get feedback about the ad it-self and the product concept.

Product ads and brochures by emails are also helpful to see the effectiveness of the designs.

The above-mentioned tests are an attempt to understand how compelling customers find this marketing material and why.

Exercise

Identify the marketing materials you want to test by considering the following options:

Webpage Evaluation:

Choose a company or a specific website and analyze one of its webpages. Identify the multiple sections, menus, and links present on the webpage. Evaluate how the webpage provides a comprehensive overview of the company, its products or services, and relevant information. Consider how the webpage facilitates visitor navigation, exploration of different sections, and access to additional pages within the website. Assess whether the webpage effectively delivers a holistic experience to visitors.

Product Video Creation:

Imagine you have a product or service that you want to showcase. Develop a script or storyboard for a product video that highlights the features, functionality, and use cases of your offering. Consider how the video can provide a more detailed and immersive view of the product, showcasing its design, performance, and user experience. Determine the purpose of the video, whether it is for marketing, sales, or educational purposes, and outline the key messages and visuals that will effectively communicate the product's benefits to the audience.

Ad Performance Analysis:

Select a web advertisement, such as a banner ad or a sponsored post, and assess its effectiveness. Evaluate the ad's design, messaging, and overall impact. Consider how the ad engages the audience and whether it effectively conveys the concept and value of the product. Reflect on the measurability of web advertisements and how they can provide valuable feedback on both the ad itself and the product concept.

Email Product Ad and Brochure Assessment:

Analyze a product ad or brochure received via email. Evaluate the design, content, and effectiveness of the email communication. Consider how well the ad or brochure conveys the product's features and benefits. Assess whether the design elements and messaging effectively capture the attention of the recipient and communicate the intended message. Reflect on the value of email marketing materials in assessing the effectiveness of design and their impact on customer engagement.

Other:

If you have any additional marketing materials that are not covered by the above categories, describe them here. This could include social media posts, email campaigns, infographics, or any other materials relevant to your marketing efforts.

6.6. Quantitative Marketing Tests

In quantitative marketing tests, various methods can be employed to gather measurable data and insights. Here are some key elements:

Landing Page: A landing page serves as a platform to describe your product or service to potential customers. Interested individuals can sign up and provide their contact information, allowing you to assess their level of interest and generate leads.

Explainer Video: An explainer video is a powerful tool to introduce your product or service. Interested viewers can then sign up to receive additional information, enabling you to gauge their engagement and intent.

Ad Campaign: Effective ad campaigns are essential for driving traffic to your landing page or explainer video. They help in attracting the attention of your target audience and directing them towards your marketing materials.

A/B Testing: A/B testing involves creating two alternative designs, such as alternative landing pages, and comparing their performance in capturing the interest and engagement of potential clients. This method helps identify which design yields a better sign-up rate.

Crowdfunding: Crowdfunding platforms like Kickstarter or Indiegogo can provide valuable insights into market demand and customer willingness to pay for your product. Launching a crowdfunding campaign allows you to gauge customer interest and validate the viability of your product or service.

By leveraging these quantitative marketing tests, you can gather valuable data, measure performance, and make informed decisions to optimize your marketing strategies and product development efforts.

Exercise

In this exercise, you will design a quantitative marketing test plan using the elements mentioned:

1. Landing Page Optimization: Choose a product or service you want to promote and create a landing page for it. Determine the key information and call-to-action you want to include. Develop a plan to measure the landing page's performance by tracking metrics such as the number of visitors, conversion rate, and lead generation. Consider using tools like Google Analytics to gather quantitative data and insights about user behavior on the landing page.

2. Explainer Video Engagement: Create an explainer video that effectively introduces your product or service. Define the main objectives of the video, such as generating interest and capturing leads. Develop a plan to measure the video's engagement by tracking metrics like views, click-through rates, and viewer interactions. Use platforms like YouTube or Vimeo, which provide analytics to assess video performance.

3. Ad Campaign Effectiveness: Design an ad campaign to drive traffic to your landing page or explainer video. Define your target audience and select appropriate advertising channels, such as social media platforms or Google Ads. Set up tracking mechanisms to measure the effectiveness of your ads, including metrics like impressions, click-through rates, and conversion rates. Use ad platforms' analytics and conversion tracking tools to gather quantitative data on campaign performance.

4. A/B Testing for Landing Pages: Create two alternative designs for your landing page. Split your incoming traffic evenly between the two versions and track key metrics like sign-up rate, bounce rate, and time spent on page. Analyze the data to determine which version performs better and generates higher user engagement. This will help you identify the most effective design elements and optimize your landing page accordingly.

5. Crowdfunding Validation: Imagine you have a product idea that you believe has market potential. Develop a crowdfunding campaign plan using platforms like Kickstarter or Indiegogo. Define the goals, target funding amount, and incentives for backers. Launch the campaign and track key metrics such as funding progress, number of backers, and engagement levels. Assess the campaign's performance to gauge market demand and validate the viability of your product concept.

6.7. Qualitative Product MVP Tests

To evaluate the viability of your Minimum Viable Product (MVP), qualitative testing methods can provide valuable insights. Here are different stages of testing[31]:

Hand Sketches: Before moving to mass production, testing the product with hand sketches can be beneficial. These simple drawings on paper allow you to gather potential customer feedback early on and validate the concept before investing further.

Wireframes: Wireframes are three-dimensional visual designs that represent the structure or skeleton of a product. They provide a more detailed representation than hand sketches, showcasing the layout and functionality without specific design elements like colors, images, or fonts. Wireframes help in assessing the overall user experience and usability of the product.

Mockups: Mockups take the testing process a step further by closely resembling the final product in terms of visual details. They incorporate design elements and provide a more realistic representation of the product's appearance and aesthetics. Mockups allow for user testing and feedback on the visual aspects, helping to refine the product's overall design.

Prototypes: Prototypes are the closest representation to the actual product. They are functional models that allow users to interact with the product and experience its features and functionalities firsthand. Prototyping provides an opportunity to gather comprehensive feedback and identify any usability or functionality issues before finalizing the product.

---

[31] Adapted from Dan Olsen's *The Lean Product Playbook: How to Innovate with Minimum Viable Products and Rapid Customer Feedback*, 2015, pg. 98-110.

Exercise

In this exercise, you will go through the process of testing a product using different qualitative methods: hand sketches, wireframes, mockups, and prototypes. Follow the steps below:

1. Hand Sketches: Choose a product idea and create hand sketches on paper to visualize its basic concept and features. Consider the overall design, functionality, and user experience. Share your hand sketches with potential customers or a focus group and gather feedback on their impressions, understanding, and suggestions for improvement.

2. Wireframes: Using design software or tools specifically for wireframing, create a three-dimensional visual representation of your product's structure and layout. Focus on capturing the main elements and interactions without specific design details like colors or images. Assess the wireframes for usability and user experience. Gather feedback from potential users or stakeholders to identify areas that may need refinement or clarification.

3. Mockups: Using graphic design software or prototyping tools, develop mockups that closely resemble the final product in terms of visual details. Incorporate design elements, such as colors, images, and fonts, to provide a realistic representation of the product's appearance and aesthetics. Conduct user testing sessions with the mockups to gather feedback on the visual aspects and overall design. Evaluate the feedback to make necessary adjustments and improvements.

4. Prototypes: Build functional prototypes of your product that users can interact with and experience firsthand. These prototypes should simulate the actual product's features and functionalities as closely as possible. Conduct user testing sessions with the prototypes to gather comprehensive feedback on usability, functionality, and overall user experience. Use the feedback to identify any issues, make iterative improvements, and validate the product before finalizing its design and moving towards mass production.

By completing this exercise, you will gain hands-on experience with different qualitative testing methods. This will enable you to validate your product concept, gather valuable user feedback, and refine the design to ensure a more successful and user-centric final product.

6.8. Quantitative Product MVP Tests

To gain valuable data-driven insights for your Minimum Viable Product (MVP), quantitative testing methods can provide valuable information. Here are some key techniques:[32]

Fake Door Test: The fake door test allows you to gauge the demand for a new feature or functionality. By including a button or a link for the proposed feature on your webpage, you can track the number of clicks it receives. Although the button may not have actual functionality, it serves as an indicator of people's interest and helps validate the demand for the feature.

Product Analytics: Product analytics provide insights into how customers interact with your product. By analyzing user behavior, you can identify which features are being used most frequently and where users spend the majority of their time. This data can help you prioritize feature development and enhance the overall user experience.

Product A/B Testing: Product A/B testing involves comparing the performance of two alternative designs or user experiences for a specific product. By randomly assigning users to different versions, you can measure and analyze their behavior and preferences. This test allows you to identify which design or experience performs better, helping you optimize your product based on user preferences.

---

[32] Adapted from Dan Olsen's *The Lean Product Playbook: How to Innovate with Minimum Viable Products and Rapid Customer Feedback, 2015, pg. 98-110.*

Exercise

In this exercise, you will simulate a testing scenario using the three methods mentioned: the Fake Door Test, Product Analytics, and Product A/B Testing. Follow the steps below:

1. Fake Door Test: Choose a specific feature or functionality you are considering adding to your product. Create a landing page or webpage that includes a button or link for this proposed feature. Share the webpage with potential users or a focus group. Track the number of clicks the button or link receives over a specific period. Analyze the results to gauge the demand and interest in the feature, even though it does not have actual functionality. Use this data to validate the demand for the feature and make informed decisions about its implementation.

2. Product Analytics: If you have an existing product, use product analytics tools such as Google Analytics or other analytics platforms to gather data on user behavior. Analyze metrics such as feature usage, time spent on different sections, and user flow within the product. Identify which features are most frequently used and where users spend the majority of their time. Based on this information, prioritize feature development and focus on enhancing the user experience in areas that receive the most attention.

3. Product A/B Testing: Select a specific aspect of your product, such as the user interface design or a feature variation, and create two alternative designs or experiences. Randomly assign users to one of the versions and track their behavior and preferences using analytics tools or user feedback. Compare the performance and user satisfaction of the two versions. Analyze the results to identify which design or experience performs better. Use this data to optimize your product based on user preferences and improve its overall effectiveness.

7 Competing to Win: SWOT Analysis and Competitive Strategy

"Strength doesn't come from what you can do.
It comes from overcoming the things you once thought you couldn't."
Rikki Rogers

7.1. Why being competitive matters?

Victor Kiam, former president of Remington, once said, "In business, the competition will bite you if you keep running; they will swallow you if you stand still."[33] Competitive analysis holds significant importance for startups. It is crucial for founders to recognize that their business idea is not entirely unique, and that competition exists in the market. Here are two reasons why being competitive matters:

Firstly, when a brilliant idea emerges, it is highly likely that multiple individuals have conceived similar concepts. It is important not to assume that you are alone in the market. Success is determined by effective marketing and swift implementation of ideas, making the best marketer and practitioner the winner in the competition.

Secondly, even if you believe your product fulfills an unmet need or surpasses existing offerings, it is essential to acknowledge that people are already addressing this need in various ways. These solutions may include substitute products, product combinations, custom solutions, or in-house alternatives. All of these become your competitors. To navigate this landscape effectively, it is crucial to analyze and understand these competitors, enabling you to develop strategies to effectively compete with them.

By understanding the competitive landscape and adopting strategies to address competitors, startups can position themselves for success and enhance their chances of gaining market share. Being aware of the competition and continuously adapting to market dynamics is vital for long-term growth and sustainability.

---

[33] Fleisher, Craig S., and Babette E. Bensoussan. *Business and competitive analysis: effective application of new and classic methods.* FT press, 2015.

7.2. Direct competition and indirect competition

Direct competition and indirect competition are two distinct types of competition that businesses face in the marketplace.[34]

Direct Competition: Direct competition refers to businesses that offer similar products or services to the same target market as your own. These are companies that are directly competing for the same customers and market share. They offer comparable solutions and compete in terms of price, features, quality, and overall value. Customers often compare these businesses and make choices based on factors such as brand reputation, customer service, and product differentiation. Direct competition can be intense, as companies strive to differentiate themselves and gain a competitive edge in the market.

Example: Two smartphone manufacturers offering similar features and specifications, targeting the same customer segment and competing for market share.

Indirect Competition: Indirect competition, on the other hand, involves businesses that offer different products or services but still fulfill similar customer needs or desires. These businesses may not be in the same industry or market segment but compete for the same consumer spending. Indirect competition arises when businesses provide alternative solutions to address a customer's underlying problem or satisfy a similar want. While they may not offer identical products, they are substitutes or alternatives that fulfill similar purposes.

Example: A cinema competing indirectly with a theme park for consumers' discretionary entertainment spending, as both options offer leisure and entertainment experiences but in different forms. Understanding both direct and indirect competition is crucial for businesses as they develop their marketing strategies and positioning. By analyzing direct competitors, companies can identify areas of differentiation and develop strategies to gain a competitive advantage. Simultaneously, recognizing indirect competition allows businesses to assess the broader market landscape and understand the various options available to customers, enabling them to refine their marketing efforts and address customer needs effectively.

---

[34] Adom, Alex Yaw, Israel Kofi Nyarko, and Gladys Narki Kumi Som. "Competitor analysis in strategic management: Is it a worthwhile managerial practice in contemporary times." *Journal of Resources Development and Management* 24.1 (2016): 116-127.

Exercise

In this exercise, you will analyze the direct and indirect competitors in your market. Follow the steps below:

Direct Competition:

1. Identify Direct Competitors: List the direct competitors in your market. These are businesses that offer products or services similar to yours and target the same customer segment.
2. Describe Competing Products: For each direct competitor, describe their product or service in detail. Outline the key features and benefits they offer to customers.
3. Evaluate Pricing: Assess the pricing strategies of each direct competitor. Note the price range of their products or services and any pricing differentiators they may have.

Indirect Competition:

1. Identify Indirect Competitors: Identify businesses that offer different products or services but fulfill similar customer needs or desires. These are indirect competitors that indirectly compete for the same customer spending.
2. Describe Indirect Competing Products: For each indirect competitor, describe their product or service and how it addresses similar customer needs. Highlight the unique features and benefits they provide.
3. Evaluate Pricing: Assess the pricing strategies of each indirect competitor. Note the price range of their products or services and any pricing differentiators they may have.

7.3. SWOT Analysis

A SWOT (Strengths, Weaknesses, Opportunities, and Threats) analysis is a strategic framework used to assess an organization's internal and external factors. Here is an extended explanation of each component with examples:

Strengths: Strengths identify what an organization excels at and what sets it apart from the competition. These can include unique capabilities, valuable resources, strong brand reputation, or a skilled workforce. For example, a technology company may have a strong research and development team, innovative products, and a well-established brand presence.

Weaknesses: Weaknesses are areas where the business needs improvement to maintain competitiveness. These can include limited market presence, outdated technology, poor customer service, or financial constraints. For instance, a retail store may struggle with outdated inventory management systems or lack a strong online presence compared to competitors.

Opportunities: Opportunities refer to favorable external factors that an organization can leverage to gain a competitive advantage. These can include emerging markets, changing consumer trends, technological advancements, or strategic partnerships. For example, a renewable energy company may identify an opportunity to expand into a growing market for sustainable energy solutions.

Threats: Threats refer to external factors that have the potential to harm an organization's performance or disrupt its operations. These can include new competitors, changing regulations, economic downturns, or shifts in customer preferences. For instance, a tourism company may face threats from political instability in a popular travel destination or the emergence of alternative vacation options.

By conducting a comprehensive SWOT analysis, organizations can identify their strengths to leverage, weaknesses to address, opportunities to capitalize on, and threats to mitigate. This analysis helps in developing strategic plans, making informed decisions, and positioning the organization for long-term success in a competitive business environment.

Exercise: SWOT Analysis

In this exercise, you will conduct a SWOT analysis for your business idea. Follow the steps below:

1. Strengths: Identify and list the organization's strengths. These are internal factors that differentiate the organization from its competitors. For each strength, provide a brief description. Examples of strengths could include a strong brand reputation, innovative product offerings, a talented workforce, or efficient internal processes.
2. Weaknesses: Identify and list the organization's weaknesses. These are internal factors that hinder the organization's competitive position. For each weakness, provide a brief description. Examples of weaknesses could include outdated technology, limited financial resources, poor customer service, or a lack of market presence.
3. Opportunities: Identify and list external opportunities that the organization can leverage for its advantage. These are favorable factors in the external environment that can support the organization's growth and competitiveness. For each opportunity, provide a brief description. Examples of opportunities could include emerging market trends, technological advancements, changing consumer preferences, or strategic partnerships.
4. Threats: Identify and list external threats that pose challenges or risks to the organization. These are factors in the external environment that may harm the organization's performance or disrupt its operations. For each threat, provide a brief description. Examples of threats could include intense competition, economic downturns, regulatory changes, or shifts in customer behavior.

8 The Marketing Advantage: Creating an Effective Plan for Your Business

"Marketing is no longer about the stuff that you make, but about the stories you tell."

Seth Godin,
All Marketers Tell Stories

8.1. Marketing Mix:

The Marketing Mix, commonly referred to as the 4 Ps of Marketing, encompasses the strategic elements of product, price, place (distribution), and promotion. These four components form the foundation of a comprehensive marketing strategy.

The 4 Ps of marketing provide a robust framework for developing a cohesive marketing plan. They are like the four legs of a chair, each one playing a crucial role. Your pricing strategy should align with your product offering, ensuring value for customers. Your distribution approach should complement your promotional efforts, ensuring the right product reaches the right place at the right time.

This marketing methodology was first introduced by E. Jerome McCarthy in his book "Basic Marketing - A Managerial Approach" in 1960. Since then, the 4 Ps of marketing have become a widely adopted framework for businesses to effectively plan and execute their marketing strategies.

8.1. Product Strategy

A company's success goes beyond its individual products; it lies in building a strong and cohesive product strategy. Just like a mother who nurtures her children, a company like Apple is more than just its MacBook Air, iPod, or iPhone. While products may change with evolving times, the entrepreneur's focus remains on creating a winning product. This is why the product strategy is a critical component of the overall marketing mix, as it sets the foundation for success.

The success of many high-tech innovations often hinges on the availability of complementary products. Take, for instance, the rise of personal computing. While the development of desktop computers played a significant role, it was the simultaneous advancements in word processing, spreadsheet, and desktop publishing software, along with the introduction of peripheral devices like laser printers, that truly fueled the personal computing revolution.[35]

Developing a product strategy involves answering key questions that shape the direction and positioning of the product:

• How do you define your product? What are its primary attributes and benefits?
• What quality level will the product adhere to?
• Will it offer customization options for customers?
• Will there be notable design distinctions? • What will be the product's name? • What range of sizes will it be available in?
• Will packaging provide added value? • Will you differentiate yourself through warranty or return policies?

Crafting strategic and thoughtful answers to these questions is vital, as it sets your product apart in the market. By focusing on these elements, entrepreneurs can ensure their product strategy aligns with market demands, customer expectations, and their overall business objectives.

---

[35] Sengupta, Sanjit. "Some approaches to complementary product strategy." *Journal of Product Innovation Management: AN INTERNATIONAL PUBLICATION OF THE PRODUCT DEVELOPMENT & MANAGEMENT ASSOCIATION* 15.4 (1998): 352-367.

Exercise: Product Strategy Analysis
In this exercise, you will analyze and define the product strategy for
your business using various criteria. Follow the steps below:

1. Product Definition: Describe your product in detail, highlighting
   its primary attributes, features, and benefits. Consider its
   intended purpose, target market, and unique selling points.
2. Quality Level: Determine the quality standards and level of
   excellence that your product will adhere to. Consider factors
   such as materials used, manufacturing processes, and quality
   control measures.
3. Customization Level: Decide the extent to which your product
   will offer customization options for customers. Consider whether
   customers can personalize aspects of the product, such as
   colors, sizes, or additional features.
4. Design Attributes: Identify the design elements that will make
   your product visually appealing and distinct. Consider factors
   such as aesthetics, ergonomics, functionality, and user
   experience.
5. Brand, Product, Model Name: Choose a compelling and
   memorable name for your product, ensuring it aligns with your
   brand identity and resonates with your target audience.
6. Sizes: Determine the range of sizes or variations that your
   product will be available in, catering to different customer
   preferences or specific market segments.
7. Packaging: Define the packaging strategy for your product,
   considering factors such as sustainability, branding, protection,
   and convenience for customers.
8. Additional Services: Explore potential additional services or
   value-added features that can enhance the overall customer
   experience and differentiate your product. This could include
   installation support, maintenance services, or after-sales
   assistance.
9. Scope of Warranty: Outline the terms and duration of the
   warranty that you will offer with your product. Consider the
   coverage, limitations, and any additional benefits that can boost
   customer confidence.
10. Return Policy: Define the policy for product returns and
    exchanges, specifying the conditions, timeframe, and procedures
    involved. Consider how to balance customer satisfaction with
    operational efficiency.

8.2. Place and Distribution Strategy:

The place and distribution strategy plays a crucial role in the overall marketing mix, and a well-executed plan can significantly impact a business's success. Wal-Mart's strategic decision to relocate its hypermarkets from city centers to suburban areas was a key factor in its achievements. By moving outside the city, Wal-Mart reduced property costs and gained more space for their stores and parking, enhancing their overall operational efficiency.

In the 1980s, companies like Apple and Dell revolutionized distribution by selling their computers directly from the factory through phone orders.[36] This direct-to-consumer approach bypassed traditional distribution channels and eliminated the need for wholesalers, resulting in increased profitability through cost savings.

Distribution strategy involves deciding channels to use to fulfil all the customer engagement roles required to reach the different segments of your target market.[37]

Developing a thoughtful distribution strategy is vital for market success. It should not be viewed as a mere operational task but rather as a strategic component. Take the time to deliberate and examine the distribution strategies employed by successful companies in your industry. By benchmarking best practices and considering logistics with a strategic mindset, you can optimize your distribution strategy to gain a competitive edge in the market.

---

[36] Dell, Michael. *Direct from Dell: Strategies that revolutionized an industry.* SAGE Publications, 2002.

[37] Cooper, Robert G. "How new product strategies impact on performance." *Journal of Product Innovation Management* 1.1 (1984): 5-18.

Exercise: Place and Distribution Strategy Analysis

In this exercise, you will analyze and develop a comprehensive place and distribution strategy for your business using various criteria. Follow the steps below:

1. Transport and Warehouse Management: Evaluate and determine the most efficient and cost-effective methods for transporting and managing your products. Consider factors such as transportation modes, logistics partners, warehouse facilities, and inventory management systems.

2. Distribution to Wholesalers and Retail Stores: Define the approach for distributing your products to wholesalers and retail stores. Determine the optimal distribution channels, partnerships, and strategies to ensure timely and efficient delivery to these intermediaries.

3. Distribution to Your Retail Store/s: Plan how you will distribute products to your own retail store/s, if applicable. Consider factors such as inventory management, stock replenishment, and delivery logistics to maintain adequate product availability for your customers.

4. Distribution by Mail: Explore the option of distributing your products through mail delivery services. Evaluate the feasibility, cost-effectiveness, and customer convenience of using mail as a distribution channel for reaching a wider audience.

5. Franchising: Consider the potential for expanding your distribution through franchising. Assess the advantages, challenges, and requirements associated with franchising your business model to leverage the expertise and resources of franchisees.

6. Inventory Levels: Determine the appropriate inventory levels to maintain, ensuring a balance between meeting customer demand and avoiding excess inventory costs. Consider factors such as lead times, demand forecasting, and safety stock requirements.

7. Vehicles for Distribution and Transportation: Select the suitable vehicles or transportation modes for product distribution. Consider factors such as load capacity, delivery distances, fuel efficiency, and environmental impact.

8. Alternative Distribution Channels: Explore alternative distribution channels beyond traditional wholesalers and retail stores. Assess opportunities for partnerships with e-commerce platforms, online marketplaces, or other non-traditional channels that align with your target market and product offerings.

9. Unconventional Distribution Channels: Consider unconventional or innovative distribution channels that can differentiate your business. Explore possibilities such as pop-up stores, mobile retail units, strategic partnerships, or direct-to-consumer models.

8.3. Promotion Strategy

A well-executed promotion strategy is often the key to success for startups. Having an exceptional product is not enough if it remains unknown to the target market. Apple's iconic "1984" advertisement made a remarkable impact on its entry into the market, catapulting the brand to global success.[38] Similarly, The Body Shop's founder, Anita Roddick, prioritized Public Relations over traditional advertising during the company's growth phase, allowing them to allocate resources to social and environmental initiatives.[39] Strategic promotion plays a pivotal role in shaping the trajectory of a startup.

The promotion strategy encompasses various elements, including the sales organization, public relations, advertising, and sales promotion.

The sales organization involves deciding whether to utilize an in-house sales force or leverage distributors' sales teams to sell your products.

Public Relations involves generating media coverage and publicity for your product through social responsibility campaigns and events.

Advertising entails creating compelling advertisements for television, print media, billboards, and social media platforms to reach your target audience effectively.

Sales promotion utilizes various media channels for a limited period to stimulate sales and consumer demand. Sales promotion activities may include contests, coupons, freebies, product samples, and more.

By strategically integrating these components into your promotion strategy, you can effectively generate awareness, drive sales, and create demand for your product or service.

---

[38] Steve Johnson, What you didn't know about Apple's '1984' Super Bowl ad, http://www.chicagotribune.com/entertainment/tv/ct-apple-1984-ad-myths-ent-0205-20170201-column.html

[39] James Bethell, Body Shop changes strategy on public relations, https://www.independent.co.uk/news/business/body-shop-changes-strategy-on-public-relations-1442891.html

Exercise: Promotion Strategy Analysis
Instructions: Evaluate and analyze the promotion strategy for your business idea by considering the following criteria. For each criterion, provide a brief description of your approach or plans.

1. Advertising Media:
      a. Billboards, Radio, and TV:
   - Describe how you will utilize these traditional advertising channels to reach your target audience effectively.
      b. Magazines and Newspapers:
   - Explain your strategy for utilizing print media to promote your product or service and engage with your target market.
      c. Google and other social media:
   - Outline your approach to leveraging digital advertising platforms, such as Google Ads and social media, to target and engage with your desired audience.
      d. Message Frequency:
   - Discuss the frequency at which you intend to communicate your promotional messages through various advertising channels.
2. Sales Force:
   - Determine the optimal number of salespeople and sales teams required to effectively promote and sell your product or service.
3. Public Relations Strategy and Campaigns:
   - Outline your plans for generating positive publicity and managing public relations to enhance your brand image and reputation.
4. Direct Marketing:
   - Explain how you will use direct marketing techniques, such as email marketing or direct mail, to target and engage potential customers.
5. Social Media Marketing Strategies:
   - Describe your strategy for leveraging social media platforms to promote your business, engage with your target audience, and build brand awareness.
6. Other Promotional Campaigns:
   - Identify any additional promotional campaigns or initiatives that you plan to implement to create buzz, generate interest, or attract customers to your business.

8.4. Pricing Strategy

Pricing strategy plays a crucial role in the success of a business as it directly impacts customer perception and purchasing decisions. Pricing moves customers and market share and that makes pricing a strategic decision.[40] Let's explore the different pricing strategies and their significance:

1. Competitive Pricing: Competitive pricing involves setting prices below, at, or above the competition. This strategy aims to position your product based on price. Setting a higher price than competitors can create the perception of superior quality, while setting a lower price can attract price-sensitive customers. Offering the same price as competitors can emphasize that your product provides additional value or features.
   - Strategy Summary: Set prices below, at, or above the competition.
   - Example: Walmart offers everyday low prices, positioning itself as an affordable option compared to competitors.

2. Customer Segment Pricing: Customer segment pricing entails setting different prices for the same or similar products based on customer characteristics or purchasing power. This strategy recognizes that different customer segments have varying willingness and ability to pay. By tailoring prices to specific segments, such as higher prices for affluent customers and lower prices for budget-conscious customers, you can capture the value perceived by each segment.
   - Strategy Summary: Set different prices for different customer segments based on their characteristics or purchasing power.
   - Example: Airlines offering different fare classes, such as economy, business, and first class, catering to customers with varying preferences and budgets.

3. Price Skimming: Price skimming involves setting a higher initial price for a new product with unique features or innovations. This strategy capitalizes on early adopters' willingness to pay a premium price for the latest offering. Over time, as competition increases or demand saturates, the price may be lowered to attract broader market segments.
   - Strategy Summary: Set a higher initial price for a new product with unique features or innovations.
   - Example: Apple launching new iPhone models at premium

---

[40] Smith, Tim. *Pricing strategy: Setting price levels, managing price discounts and establishing price structures.* Cengage Learning, 2011.

prices to capture early adopters and technology enthusiasts.

4. Penetration Pricing: Penetration pricing focuses on setting a lower initial price to quickly gain market share and attract existing customers. By offering a more affordable alternative, this strategy aims to capture a significant customer base and build brand loyalty. Once a strong market position is established, prices may be adjusted to generate higher profits.
   - Strategy Summary: Set a lower initial price to gain market share and attract existing customers.
   - Example: Amazon's Kindle devices priced competitively to penetrate the e-reader market and establish a large customer base.

When choosing a pricing strategy, it is important to consider factors such as the target market, product differentiation, production costs, and competitive landscape. Additionally, discounts, coupons, rebates, and sales campaigns can be employed to stimulate demand and incentivize purchases.

Selecting the right pricing strategy requires a careful evaluation of market dynamics, customer preferences, and business objectives. By effectively implementing a pricing strategy, businesses can optimize their revenue, establish competitive positioning, and drive long-term growth.

Exercise
Consider the following criteria for pricing strategies and answer the questions accordingly:

1. Competitive Pricing:
   - Identify two or more competitors in your market.
   - Determine whether you will set your prices below, at, or above the competition.
   - Explain the reasons behind your chosen pricing approach.

2. Customer Segment Pricing:
   - Identify two distinct customer segments for your product or service.
   - Decide on different price levels for each segment based on their characteristics or purchasing power.
   - Justify your pricing differentiation for each customer segment.

3. Price Skimming:
   - Imagine launching a new product with unique features or innovations.
   - Determine an initial higher price for this product.
   - Explain why you have chosen price skimming as the pricing strategy for this particular product.

4. Market Penetration Pricing:
    - Suppose you want to quickly gain market share and attract existing customers.
    - Decide on a lower initial price for your product to achieve market penetration.
    - Describe how this pricing strategy will help you capture a significant customer base.
5. Allowances:
    - Determine whether you will offer any rebates or allowances for distributors.
    - Explain the purpose and benefits of providing these allowances to distributors.

6. Payment Terms:
    - Decide on the payment terms you will offer to customers, such as credit or specific payment methods.
    - Justify your choice of payment terms based on customer preferences or industry norms.

7. Discounts:
    - Determine if you will provide any discounts for customers.
    - Explain the conditions or criteria for receiving these discounts and how they will benefit both the customers and your business.

8. List Prices:
    - Set the initial list prices for your product or service.
    - Explain the factors considered and the rationale behind your pricing decisions.

9 The Supply Chain Solution: Managing Your Business's Resources

"Leaders win through logistics. Vision, sure. Strategy, yes. But when you go to war, you need to have both toilet paper and bullets at the right place at the right time. In other words, you must win through superior logistics."

Tom Peters
Business Guru

9.1. Sourcing Strategy - Supply Management

The sourcing of your products plays a crucial role in determining the quality of your offerings and the overall success of your business.[41] Take McDonald's, for example. The quality of their meat, buns, and potatoes is instrumental in their business success. Similarly, Starbucks relies heavily on its suppliers to maintain the consistency and excellence of their coffee and related products. Ensuring a stable and reliable supply chain is essential for maintaining customer satisfaction and loyalty.

Supply management encompasses four critical dimensions:

1. Price: Price is a vital consideration as it directly impacts your profitability. Finding suppliers that offer competitive pricing while maintaining quality is essential for optimizing your costs.
2. Order Fulfillment: The capacity, ease, and speed of order fulfillment are crucial factors to consider. A reliable supplier should be able to provide a large quantity of goods when needed, with an efficient and streamlined ordering process. Timely delivery is critical to ensure you always have sufficient stock to meet customer demands.
3. Quality: Consistency in product quality is paramount to your business success. Fluctuations or inconsistencies in product quality can negatively impact customer satisfaction and lead to a loss of customers. Selecting suppliers who maintain strict quality control measures is vital for delivering exceptional products to your customers.
4. Payment Terms: Payment terms also play a significant role in the sourcing process. Whether it's advance payment requirements or payment within a specified timeframe, such as 60 days after order placement, the payment terms directly impact your financials and cash flow management.

You can establish a robust sourcing strategy that ensures the availability of high-quality products, optimal pricing, efficient order fulfillment, and favorable payment terms.

---

[41] Talluri, Srinivas, and Ram Narasimhan. "A methodology for strategic sourcing." *European journal of operational research* 154.1 (2004): 236-250.

9.2. Supplier Evaluation:

Supply chain management that involves assessing and selecting suppliers based on various criteria. The following criteria are commonly used for supplier evaluation:

1. Quality: Assessing the quality of the supplier's products or services is crucial. High-quality products or services are essential for maintaining customer satisfaction and meeting the standards of your business.

2. Ease of Order: Evaluating the ease of placing orders with a supplier is important for streamlining your procurement process. A supplier with a user-friendly and efficient ordering system can help reduce administrative burden and improve overall operational efficiency.

3. Capacity: Evaluating the supplier's capacity refers to assessing their ability to meet your demands in terms of quantity and volume. A supplier should have the necessary resources, infrastructure, and production capabilities to fulfill your orders effectively.

4. Speed: Supplier responsiveness and lead times are critical factors in ensuring timely delivery of goods or services. Assessing a supplier's speed in processing and delivering orders is crucial for meeting customer expectations and maintaining a competitive edge.

5. Payment: Evaluating the supplier's payment terms and conditions is important for managing your financial obligations effectively. Consider factors such as payment methods, credit terms, and any discounts or incentives offered by the supplier.

6. Price: Price competitiveness is a significant consideration in supplier evaluation. Analyzing the supplier's pricing structure and comparing it with market standards can help you ensure cost-effectiveness and maximize profitability.

7. Reputation: Assessing the supplier's reputation involves considering their track record and customer feedback. A supplier with a positive reputation for reliability, trustworthiness, and ethical business practices is more likely to be a valuable partner.

8. Consistency: Evaluating the supplier's consistency refers to their ability to consistently deliver high-quality products or services over time. Consistency is crucial for maintaining product standards and meeting customer expectations.

Exercise: Supplier Evaluation

Evaluate the following suppliers based on the criteria of quality, ease of order, capacity, speed, payment, price, reputation, and consistency. Assign a rating from 1 to 5 (1 being the lowest and 5 being the highest) for each criterion, indicating the supplier's performance.

Supplier A:
- Quality:
- Ease of Order:
- Capacity:
- Speed:
- Payment:
- Price:
- Reputation:
- Consistency:

Supplier B:
- Quality:
- Ease of Order:
- Capacity:
- Speed:
- Payment:
- Price:
- Reputation:
- Consistency:

Supplier C:
- Quality:
- Ease of Order:
- Capacity:
- Speed:
- Payment:
- Price:
- Reputation:
- Consistency:

After assigning ratings for each criterion, analyze the results and identify the strengths and weaknesses of each supplier. Consider the overall performance of each supplier and determine which one would be the most suitable choice for your business based on your specific requirements and priorities.

9.3. Technology Strategy

Technology plays a vital role in shaping the performance and efficiency of a business.[42] It encompasses the machinery, tools, and methods used in operations, which can significantly impact productivity and cost-effectiveness.

The integration of technology into business operations can lead to increased efficiency and improved outcomes. For example, the use of robotics in manufacturing can streamline production processes and reduce labor costs. In warehouses, automated systems and robotics can enhance inventory management and accelerate order fulfillment. In office settings, computer programs and software applications can automate repetitive tasks and streamline workflows, leading to higher productivity and time savings. Additionally, self-service technologies, such as online platforms and mobile apps, are revolutionizing customer interactions and replacing traditional call centers.

When considering technology implementation, a startup should assess its primary technologies, which are essential for conducting its core business operations. These may include specialized software, manufacturing equipment, or communication systems tailored to the company's unique needs. Additionally, supplemental technologies, such as project management tools, collaboration platforms, or customer relationship management software, can support day-to-day operations and enhance overall efficiency.

By carefully selecting and utilizing appropriate technologies, startups can gain a competitive edge, optimize their operations, and meet the evolving demands of the market. It is crucial to continually evaluate and update technology strategies to leverage the latest advancements and remain innovative in an ever-changing business landscape.

---

[42] Ford, David. "Develop your technology strategy." *Long range planning* 21.5 (1988): 85-95.

Exercise: Technology Choices

Consider the critical and supplemental technologies that you will use in your business. For each technology, provide a brief description, list the advantages and disadvantages, and estimate the associated costs.

Technology Name:

Brief Description:

Advantages:

Disadvantages:

Cost Estimate:

9.4. Strategic Alliance and Partnerships

Strategic alliances play a crucial role in the growth and success of businesses. By forming alliances, companies can leverage each other's strengths, resources, and expertise to achieve common business goals. There are various types of strategic alliances, including co-marketing, co-production, co-development, and cooperative arrangements.

Co-marketing alliances involve collaborating with another company to jointly promote products or services. By pooling marketing efforts and resources, both companies can reach a wider audience, increase brand visibility, and generate more sales.

Co-production alliances occur when two or more companies collaborate to produce goods or services together. This partnership allows companies to share production facilities, equipment, or expertise, resulting in increased efficiency, cost savings, and improved product quality.

Co-development alliances involve joint research and development efforts between companies. By combining their knowledge, research capabilities, and resources, companies can accelerate innovation, develop new products or technologies, and gain a competitive edge in the market.

Cooperative arrangements encompass various forms of collaboration, such as sharing distribution channels, logistics, or supply chain resources. Companies can benefit from increased market reach, improved distribution efficiency, and reduced costs by aligning their supply or distribution strategies with complementary partners.

For example, Company A may enter into a strategic alliance with Company B, where Company A sells the product while Company B produces it. The market success of Company A's product will have a positive impact on the sales of Company B, creating a mutually beneficial relationship.

Strategic alliances offer companies opportunities for growth, expansion, and increased competitiveness by leveraging the strengths and resources of partnering organizations. By working together, companies can achieve synergies, mitigate risks, and enhance their overall performance in the market.

Exercise

In the exercise, you should identify potential partners relevant to your specific business field and describe the collaboration activity or initiative that aligns with your business goals and objectives.

Collaboration Field: [Enter your business field]

Partner: [List potential companies that could be a good fit for an alliance]

Collaboration Activity: [Describe the specific collaboration activity or initiative that could be undertaken with each potential partner]

10 Vision and Strategy: Developing Your Business Plan for Success

Good leaders have vision and inspire others to help them turn vision into reality. Great leaders create more leaders, not followers. Great leaders have vision, share vision, and inspire others to create their own."

Roy T. Bennett,
The Light in the Heart

10.1. Vision

A vision statement serves as a guiding force that outlines the desired future state of a company. It defines where you envision your company to be in the long term and provides a clear sense of direction.

Vision is often confused with the similar constructs of organization mission, philosophy and values, strategy, and goals.[43]

A compelling vision statement is bold and inspirational, capturing the essence of what your organization aspires to achieve.

A strong vision statement includes a measurable definition of success and a compelling call to action, inspiring both employees and stakeholders to work towards its realization.

For example, Amazon's vision statement is "To be the Earth's most customer-centric company, where customers can find and discover anything they might want to buy online." Amazon's vision statement is concise and impactful, reflecting their unwavering commitment to customer satisfaction and their determination to offer a wide range of products and services through their online platform.

---

[43] Levin, Ira M. "Vision revisited: Telling the story of the future." *The Journal of Applied Behavioral Science* 36.1 (2000): 91-107.

Exercise

In this exercise, through a series of questions, you will articulate your vision, identify key measures of success, and determine the primary actions required to bring your vision to life.

- What achievements do you envision for the future?
- How will you measure progress towards your vision?
- What key steps or initiatives will you undertake to realize your vision?
- What is your vision statement, summarizing the desired future state of your company in a clear and inspiring way?

10.2. Mission Statement

If vision is the desired destination, then the mission statement serves as the roadmap for reaching that destination. While the vision statement outlines where the organization wants to go, the mission statement defines how it will get there. It encapsulates the purpose and values of the organization, providing guidance and direction for its actions and decisions.

For example, let's consider Harley-Davidson. Their vision is to be the leader in the motorcycle industry, providing an exceptional riding experience and fostering a strong community of motorcycle enthusiasts. Their mission statement, "We fulfill dreams through the experience of motorcycling, by providing motorcyclists and the general public with an expanding line of motorcycles and branded products and services in selected market segments,"[44] showcases how they aim to achieve this vision.

In this context, the mission statement of Harley-Davidson highlights their commitment to fulfilling the dreams of their customers through the experience of motorcycling. It emphasizes their focus on providing an expanding line of motorcycles, as well as branded products and services, to cater to the needs and desires of their target market segments. By narrowing their field of activity to motorcycles and emphasizing the experience of motorcycling, Harley-Davidson differentiates itself from other automotive businesses and demonstrates a clear understanding of their unique value proposition.

By aligning their mission statement with their vision, Harley-Davidson sets a clear direction for their organization. It guides their decisions and actions, ensuring that they are consistently working towards their goal of delivering exceptional motorcycle experiences and building a strong community of riders.

In summary, the mission statement serves as a powerful tool for organizations to articulate how they will achieve their vision. It communicates their core purpose, values, and strategic focus, guiding their efforts and inspiring stakeholders to rally behind their shared goals. The majority of corporate mission statements lack substance and hold little value. They are often filled with empty clichés, such as pledges to uphold high standards of professionalism and ethical behavior. Many of these statements state basic necessities as objectives, such as the aim

---

[44] Dan McCarthy, Mission Statement

https://www.thebalancecareers.com/strategic-plan-elements-2276139

to achieve a sufficient level of profit. This is comparable to an individual stating that their mission is to breathe adequately.[45]

---

[45] Ackoff, Russel L. "Mission statements." *Planning Review* (1987).

Exercise: Crafting Your Mission Statement
Instructions:
1. Reflect on your vision for your business or organization and consider what you will do to achieve that vision. Write down your response to the question: "What will you do to achieve your vision?"
2. Next, think about what you will avoid doing to achieve your vision. Identify any practices, behaviors, or approaches that you believe would hinder your progress towards your vision. Write down your response to the question: "What will you avoid doing to achieve your vision?"
3. Consider how you will go about implementing your strategies and actions to achieve your vision. Think about the specific steps, approaches, or methods you will employ. Write down your response to the question: "How will you do it?"
4. Finally, synthesize your responses into a concise mission statement. Capture the essence of your purpose, strategies, and values in a clear and inspiring statement. Write down your mission statement.

10.3. Action Plan

A dynamic action plan is crucial for the success of any business. It involves setting goals and priorities that align with your vision. An action plan helps optimize the use of your time and enables you to focus on essential tasks efficiently.

Effective goals are clear, stating what you aim to achieve, when you intend to accomplish it (timeframe), how you will do it, and who is responsible for its execution. Each goal should be specific and measurable, allowing you to track progress and success.

An action plan can be implemented across various aspects of your business, including human resources, marketing, operations, supply management, financial management, and more. While not all plans may come to fruition, they serve as valuable guides that propel you toward your vision. Implemented plans provide insights into successful strategies and areas for improvement. The best action plans are not rigid but rather dynamic, allowing for adaptability and change as needed.

Exercise: Action Plan for the 1st Quarter of Your Business
In this exercise, identify the key tasks or projects that need to be accomplished during the 1st quarter of your business. For each task or project, define a measurable goal that can be tracked for progress. Set a deadline for completion and assign a responsible person who will be accountable for its execution.

Task or Project:
Measurable Goal
Deadline:
Responsible Person:

10.4. Milestones

Milestones serve as important reference points along the journey of a business. They can be compared to the historical use of milestones in the Roman Empire, where they provided reassurance to travelers about their progress and distance to their destination.

In the context of business, milestones are specific targets that mark significant points along a timeline. They act as indicators that a particular phase or stage has been completed, and a new phase is about to begin. Milestones often represent key events, achievements, or deliverables within a project or business plan. They can include important dates, external reviews or inputs, budget assessments, or other significant checkpoints.

By setting and tracking milestones, businesses can effectively monitor progress, stay on track, and assess the overall success of their initiatives. Milestones serve as guideposts, ensuring that the business is moving in the right direction and making tangible progress towards its goals and objectives.

Exercise: Your Business Milestones
In this exercise, you will identify and define important milestones for your business across different fields or departments. These milestones will serve as key reference points to mark significant achievements and track progress within your business. For each milestone, indicate the business field or department it relates to and the target completion date.

Milestone:
Business Field / Department:
The Target Completion Date:

11 Corporate Culture: Building Your Business Philosophy and Values

"A highly developed values system is like a compass. It serves as a guide to point you in the right direction when you are lost."

Idowu Koyenikan,
Wealth for All: Living a Life of Success at the Edge of Your Ability

11.1. Corporate Philosophy

When starting a business, many entrepreneurs have a product idea in mind. However, solely focusing on the product may leave them unprepared to navigate obstacles along their journey. To stay on track, entrepreneurs need guiding principles that form the foundation of their business. The most successful entrepreneurs of today's largest corporations had a clear corporate philosophy from the very beginning.

For instance, Whole Foods has established core values that shape their corporate philosophy.[46] These values serve as guiding principles to make decisions at every crossroad:

- We Sell the Highest Quality Natural and Organic Foods
- We Satisfy and Delight Our Customers
- We Promote Team Member Growth and Happiness
- We Practice Win-Win Partnerships with Our Suppliers
- We are part of an interdependent business ecosystem.
- We Create Profits and Prosperity
- We Care About our Community and the Environment

A well-defined corporate philosophy serves several purposes. It helps shape the corporate culture and guides employees in their decision-making process.[47] Additionally, it communicates the values of the company to both internal and external stakeholders. By providing a shared starting point for decision-making, a corporate philosophy ensures that all employees are aligned and working towards a common goal.

---

[46] Whole Foods Core Values, https://www.wholefoodsmarket.com/mission-values/core-values

[47] Sampson Quain, Examples of Corporate Philosophy, http://smallbusiness.chron.com/examples-corporate-philosophy-37868.html

Exercise: Corporate Philosophy and Values Assessment
Instructions: For each domain listed below, reflect on your company's
corporate philosophy and values. Identify the core values and guiding
principles that your company upholds in relation to each domain.
Consider how these values shape your business decisions and practices.
Write a brief description for each domain, highlighting the key values
and principles associated with it.

1. Customers:
    *   Core Values:

2. Products and Services:
    *   Core Values:

3. Innovation:
    *   Core Values:

4. People (Stakeholders):
    *   Core Values:

5. Suppliers:
    *   Core Values:

6. Environment:
    *   Core Values:

7. Profit:
    *   Core Values:

8. Leadership and Management:
    *   Core Values:

State Your Corporate Philosophy:

12 Creating Your Identity: Branding and Marketing Your Business

"Design is the silent ambassador of your brand."
Paul Rand

12. 1. Guidelines for Choosing a Company Name

Choosing the right name for your company can provide a competitive advantage and contribute to its success. Consider the following principles when brainstorming and selecting a company name:

1. Easy to Spell: Avoid names that are difficult to spell or prone to confusion. A straightforward and easily recognizable name facilitates brand recognition and recall. (Example: Food2Go)
2. Catchy and Memorable: Select a name that captures attention and leaves a lasting impression. A catchy name can pique curiosity and generate interest in your brand. (Example: BestBuy)
3. Scalability: Ensure that the chosen name has the potential to grow with your business. Avoid names that may limit your company's future expansion or evolution. (Example: Brown Computers)
4. Meaningful and Benefit-oriented: Choose a name that holds significance and conveys a clear benefit or value proposition to your target audience. This helps customers understand what your company offers. (Example: Whole Foods)
5. Avoid Generic Names: Steer clear of generic names that lack distinction and fail to convey a unique identity. Stand out by selecting a name that has character and sets your company apart. (Example: Books)
6. Trademark Availability: Check if the name is available for trademark registration to protect your brand identity and prevent potential legal conflicts. (Example: America)
7. Appeal to Target Customers: Consider the preferences and interests of your target customers. Select a name that resonates with your desired audience and aligns with their values and expectations. (Example: American Girl - a doll company; Dollar Tree - a convenience store)
8. Concise and Clear: Avoid long or confusing names that may be challenging for customers to remember or understand. Keep it simple and straightforward. (Example: Boston Market - a chicken restaurant)
9. Secure the ".com" Domain: In today's digital age, having the corresponding ".com" domain for your company name is crucial for online presence and credibility.
10. Creativity: Combine familiarity with uniqueness to create a memorable and distinctive name. Consider incorporating elements that are already familiar to your potential customers while adding a touch of originality. (Example: Apple - the image of Adam and Eve, symbolizing breaking conventions)

11. Reflect Your Business Philosophy: Choose a name that aligns with your business philosophy and core values. This creates a strong connection between your brand and its mission. (Example: BestBuy)
12. Geographical References: Incorporating geographical names can give the impression of a larger company and broaden your market appeal. (Example: American Life)

Exercise: Choosing a Company Name
Instructions: Imagine you are starting a new business and need to choose a name that represents your brand effectively. Use the following criteria to brainstorm potential names and evaluate their suitability. Write down your ideas and assess them based on the given guidelines.

Name Ideas:
1.
2.
3.
4.
5.

Evaluation:
• Assess each name idea based on the provided guidelines.
• Determine if the name meets the criteria and reflects your brand's identity effectively.
• Eliminate names that do not align with the guidelines or your business goals.
• Rank the remaining names based on their suitability and potential impact.

Reflection:
• Reflect on the remaining name options and their implications for your business.
• Consider how each name may resonate with your target audience and differentiate your brand.
• Select the most suitable name that embodies your vision, values, and market positioning.

Choosing a company name is an important decision, so take your time and consider the impact it will have on your brand's identity and future growth.

12.2. Logo Design Guideline

A well-designed logo can play a crucial role in the success of a startup. Take Coca-Cola's iconic logo, for example, which has become synonymous with the company's brand. When creating your logo, consider the following principles[48] as a guideline:

1. Reflect Your Business Brand: Ensure that your logo reflects the essence and values of your business. It should visually convey the personality and identity of your brand.
2. Unique and Perceivable: Your logo should stand out and be easily recognizable to your target audience. It should have a distinctive and memorable design that sets it apart from competitors.
3. Keep it Simple: Aim for simplicity in your logo design. The most effective logos are often those that have evolved over time to become streamlined and refined. Avoid excessive complexity that may diminish visual impact.
4. Strategic Use of Colors: Select colors that align with your business philosophy and positioning. Colors evoke emotions and associations, so choose them strategically to convey the desired message and create a harmonious visual identity.
5. Scalable and Versatile: Ensure your logo design can be scaled up or down without losing its visual integrity. It should be adaptable to various formats and mediums, such as business cards, websites, or promotional materials, and retain its aesthetic appeal.
6. Effective in Black and White: Test your logo's design by rendering it in black and white. A strong logo should still retain its impact and clarity without relying on color.
7. Memorable and Timeless: Strive for a logo design that leaves a lasting impression on viewers. It should be memorable and able to withstand the test of time, avoiding trendy elements that may quickly become outdated.
8. Audience Appropriateness: Consider your target audience when designing your logo. It should resonate with their preferences, expectations, and values, ensuring relevance and connection.
9. Conceptual Relevance: If applicable, incorporate relevant visual elements or symbols that convey the unique characteristics or benefits of your product or service. For example, if your product is related to memory, consider using an animal known for its sharp memory, like an elephant (e.g., Evernote).

---

[48] Adapted from Roy Miller. 6 Basic Principles Of Logo Design. https://www.designhill.com/design-blog/basic-principles-logo-design/.

Exercise: Logo Design

In this exercise, you will be creating a logo for your business or company. Follow the steps below to design a logo that effectively represents your brand:

Choose an Animal or Object: Select an animal or object that symbolizes your business or company. Consider its characteristics, traits, or associations that align with your brand identity.

Relevant Colors: Choose colors that are relevant to your business. Think about the emotions, values, or attributes you want to convey. Research color psychology to understand how different colors can evoke specific reactions or perceptions.

Universal Symbols: Identify universal symbols that represent the benefits or unique aspects of your products and services. These symbols should have a broad understanding and resonate with your target audience.

Distinctive Visual Aspects: Explore the distinctive visual aspects of your business or industry. Look for elements, shapes, or patterns that can visually differentiate your logo and make it memorable.

13 Building Your Team: Strategies for Attracting and Retaining Talent

"In fact, leaders of companies that go from good to great start not with 'where' but with 'who.' They start by getting the right people on the bus, the wrong people off the bus, and the right people in the right seats. And they stick with that discipline—first the people, then the direction— no matter how dire the circumstances."

Jim Collins,
Good to Great

13.1. Advisory Board

An advisory board is a select group of advisors who provide guidance and expertise to a startup. In the world of startups, knowledge is a valuable asset. While founders may excel in their product domain, they may lack expertise in crucial business areas such as accounting, marketing, social media, human resources, and finance. This is where an advisory board can play a vital role by offering their specialized knowledge, advice, and network.

Building an advisory board allows startups to tap into the wisdom and experience of individuals who have already mastered the intricacies of a specific field. Instead of spending years learning the tips and tricks, you can leverage the insights of your advisors to accelerate your growth. Whether it's strategic guidance, industry connections, or navigating complex challenges, the advisory board can provide valuable perspectives.

Members of the advisory board can come from various backgrounds, including active professional managers in corporations, experienced accountants, finance experts, or individuals who are temporarily available due to retirement or career transitions. The number of advisory board members and their areas of expertise should be tailored to the specific needs of the business. For instance, the advisory board composition for a service-oriented company may differ from that of a production-focused company.

Exercise: Advisory Board

List the members of the advisory board. Include a brief description of backgrounds and organizational roles.

Domain
Accounting and Taxes
Finance
Management
Marketing
Human Resources
Law
Technology
Social Media
Media Relations
Other

13.2. Creating a People Strategy

One of the defining factors in a startup is the people strategy. Apple became a successful company be-cause, from the very start, they tried to hire the best people available in the world. McDonald's founder, Ray Kroc, designed a business for ordinary employ-ees. Starbucks is a coffee shop chain, but it is a com-pany more about people. Starbucks gives all the em-ployees health insurance and supports them in at-taining higher education. So, usually, entrepreneurs believe that their success is a function of a brilliant product. However, they need to keep in mind that anything in the company is the work of employees. They run the business. Your employees will deter-mine if you will be a start-up, or a start-down. You should think about your people strategy. When we use the word strategy, it should be unique and creative. Regarding your people strategy, you should develop plans for hiring, rewarding, compensating, training, promoting, and creating a culture.

Exercise: Developing a People Strategy
The success of a startup is heavily influenced by its people strategy. Companies like Apple, McDonald's, and Starbucks have demonstrated the power of investing in their employees from the early stages. While entrepreneurs often focus on their product or service, it is essential to recognize that the collective effort of employees drives the company's success.

Creating an effective people strategy requires thoughtful consideration and creativity. It encompasses various aspects, including hiring, rewarding, compensating, training, promoting, and fostering a positive company culture.

Hiring: Develop a strategic approach to attract and select top talent that aligns with your company's values and goals. Define the qualities and skills you seek in candidates to build a high-performing team.

Reward and Compensation: Design a comprehensive rewards system that recognizes and incentivizes employees' contributions. Consider both monetary and non-monetary benefits to create a competitive and engaging work environment.

Training and Development: Implement a robust training program that equips employees with the skills and knowledge needed to excel in their roles. Foster a culture of continuous learning and provide opportunities for professional growth.

Promotion: Establish clear criteria and a transparent process for promoting employees based on performance, potential, and alignment with company objectives. Encourage internal career progression and leadership development.

Culture: Cultivate a positive and inclusive work culture that values diversity, collaboration, and innovation. Define the core values and behaviors that guide employee interactions and shape the overall company culture.

13.3. Management Team

The management team plays a vital role in the effective functioning of the company. Each member has specific responsibilities and contributes to the overall success of the startup. Here are the key roles within a management team:

Chief Executive Officer (CEO): The CEO is responsible for setting the corporate strategy, establishing key business relationships, hiring critical personnel, and addressing major challenges faced by the startup. They provide leadership and direction to the entire organization.

Chief Operations Officer (COO): The COO oversees the day-to-day operations of the company, including production, procurement, logistics, and other operational functions. They ensure the smooth execution of business processes and manage resources efficiently.

Chief Technology Officer (CTO): The CTO plays a crucial role in shaping the technological aspects of the company. They are responsible for selecting and developing the appropriate technology infrastructure, driving innovation, and ensuring the company stays up-to-date with the latest advancements in their industry.

Chief Marketing Officer (CMO): The CMO develops and implements the marketing strategy of the company. They are in charge of creating the brand identity, devising advertising and social media campaigns, addressing packaging issues, and driving customer engagement and satisfaction.

Chief Finance Officer (CFO): The CFO oversees the financial management of the company. They develop financial strategies, create budgets, monitor cash flow, and ensure compliance with financial regulations. The CFO plays a critical role in managing the company's financial health and ensuring its long-term sustainability.

Exercise: Your Management Team

Who will be your management team members?

Position and Name

CEO
COO
CTO
CMO
CFO

13.4. Organizational Structure

An organizational structure provides a framework for defining the hierarchy, authority relationships, and division of responsibilities within a company. It determines how roles, functions, and teams are organized and how information flows within the organization.

In a startup, having a clear and well-defined organizational structure is crucial for efficient operations and effective decision-making. It allows for the development of specialized departments and positions, promoting collaboration and accountability.

Example

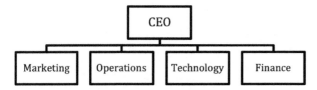

The organizational chart visually represents the structure of the company, showing the different levels of management, departments, teams, and their relationships. It provides a bird's eye view of the organization, helping stakeholders understand the reporting lines and overall framework of the company.

By creating an organizational structure, startups can enhance communication, streamline processes, and foster a sense of clarity and direction among employees. It enables efficient coordination, improves workflow, and facilitates the achievement of organizational goals.

Developing a sound organizational structure is an ongoing process that should align with the company's objectives, strategies, and growth plans. It ensures that responsibilities are clearly defined, promotes efficient resource allocation, and enables the company to adapt and scale as it evolves.

Exercise: Organizational Structure

Draw your organizational chart below.

13.5. Staff Plan

A staff plan is a crucial component of building and managing a company's workforce. It involves determining the organizational structure and identifying the positions required to effectively run the business. Each position within the company should be clearly defined, outlining its purpose, responsibilities, and the skills and qualifications needed.

Creating a comprehensive staff plan allows for better resource allocation and workforce management. It helps in predicting the costs associated with the operations of the business, including salaries, benefits, office space, equipment, and other necessary resources. By estimating these costs, a company can develop a budget and ensure that sufficient resources are allocated to support the staffing needs.

The staff plan also supports strategic decision-making related to hiring, training, and talent acquisition. It enables the identification of skill gaps and the determination of recruitment strategies to attract the right individuals for each position. Additionally, the staff plan serves as a reference for workforce development, career progression, and succession planning.

By having a well-defined staff plan in place, a company can effectively align its human resources with its organizational goals and objectives. It facilitates the efficient functioning of the business, promotes a productive work environment, and supports the growth and success of the organization.

Exercise: Your Staff Plan
Create your staff plan using the below format.
Department:
Job Title/ Qualifications:
Annual Salary / Cost:
Assigned Personnel:

14 Pitch Perfect: Crafting a Compelling Business Proposal

"If you cannot explain it simply, you don't understand well enough."
Albert Einstein

14.1. Pitching Your Business Idea

Pitching is a critical element of presenting your business idea to potential investors or partners. It is an opportunity to convey your vision, explain your product or service, and showcase the value and potential of your venture. Different formats, such as an elevator pitch or a video pitch, allow you to deliver your message effectively within a limited timeframe. The primary objective of a pitch is to generate interest and secure funding for your company.[49] To achieve this, your pitch should cover key aspects:

1. Company and Product Overview: Provide a concise and compelling description of your company, highlighting its mission, goals, and the core features of your product or service. Clearly communicate the problem your offering addresses and the benefits it provides to customers.
2. Solution and Competitive Advantage: Present your solution to the identified problem, emphasizing how it stands out from existing alternatives. Clearly articulate the unique selling points and competitive advantages that set your business apart in the market.
3. Financial Opportunity: Outline the potential returns and benefits for investors. Explain the revenue model, growth projections, and market potential of your business. Highlight the market size, target audience, and potential for scalability.
4. Funding Request: Clearly state the amount of investment you are seeking to fund your company's growth and expansion. Justify the funding requirement by aligning it with your business plan and explaining how the investment will be utilized to achieve key milestones and generate returns for investors.

Crafting a compelling pitch requires careful planning and practice. Tailor your presentation to the specific audience and adapt it to different formats or time constraints. Focus on capturing attention, conveying your passion, and showcasing the potential of your business idea to inspire confidence and generate interest from potential investors or partners.

---

[49] Alan Gleeson,The Business Pitch, http://articles.bplans.co.uk/starting-a-business/the-business-pitch/407

Exercise Pitch Preparation:
Once you have completed the following steps, you can use the information to structure your pitch and practice delivering it in a concise, compelling, and confident manner. Tailoring your pitch to the specific needs and interests of your audience is crucial.

Step 1: Business Overview
- Describe your business in a concise manner, highlighting its key aspects, such as industry, target market, and unique value proposition.

Step 2: Product or Service Description
- Clearly articulate the core features and benefits of your product or service, highlighting what makes it innovative or superior compared to existing solutions in the market.

Step 3: Customer Problem
- Identify the specific problem or pain point that your target customers are facing. Explain why it is significant and how it affects their lives or businesses.

Step 4: Your Solution
- Present your solution as the answer to the customer problem. Highlight the key features, functionalities, or advantages that make your solution stand out from competitors.

Step 5: Investor Benefits
- Outline the potential benefits and returns that investors can expect from investing in your business. Emphasize the growth potential, market demand, and revenue projections that make your venture an attractive investment opportunity.

Step 6: Funding Request
- Specify the amount of investment you are seeking to support your business growth and expansion plans. Justify the funding requirement by linking it to the milestones and objectives outlined in your business plan.

15 Financial Forecasting: How to Create Accurate Projections for Your Business

"If you can look into the seeds of time and say which grain will grow and which will not, speak, then, to me."
William Shakespeare,
Macbeth

15.1. Funding Your Start-up:

When it comes to funding your business idea and getting your startup off the ground, there are various options available to consider:[50]

Self-Funding: Using your own money, savings, or personal earnings to finance your business is a common approach. You can also explore the possibility of selling personal assets. However, it's important to recognize that if the company faces financial challenges or fails, you may risk losing your personal investment.

Friends and Family: Borrowing money from friends and family members can be an initial source of funding. They may be willing to support your venture and help you get your company up and running. However, it's crucial to establish clear terms and repayment plans to maintain healthy relationships and avoid potential conflicts.

Trade Equity or Services: Consider leveraging your skills and expertise to acquire necessary services or resources. For example, as a chef in need of a professional kitchen, you can offer to provide catering services in exchange for free use of the kitchen facilities during off-hours.

Small Business Loans: Some banks and financial institutions offer loans specifically tailored for small businesses. However, qualifying for a loan may require collateral and a solid business plan. Be prepared to provide detailed financial projections and demonstrate your ability to repay the loan.

Small Business Grants: Non-profit organizations and government agencies often provide grants to support small businesses. While the grants may be relatively small, they can provide valuable initial funding to kickstart your venture.

Accelerators: Consider joining a business accelerator or incubator program. These organizations offer a range of support services, mentorship, and funding opportunities for startups. They can provide access to capital, office space, and valuable resources to help your business grow.

Contests: Participating in business idea and plan contests can provide a chance to secure funding for your startup. Even if you don't win, these contests offer an excellent opportunity to refine your business idea and pitch, as well as gain exposure to potential investors.

---

[50] https://www.startupgrind.com/blog/9-realistic-ways-to-fund-your-startup/

Crowdfunding: Crowdfunding platforms like Kickstarter and Indiegogo allow entrepreneurs to showcase their ideas and attract funding from a large pool of contributors. This option is particularly suitable if you have a compelling and marketable idea and can create an engaging crowdfunding campaign.

Carefully consider each funding option based on your specific needs, resources, and goals. It may be beneficial to explore a combination of funding sources to secure the necessary capital to launch and grow your startup.

15.2. Sales Forecast

Sales forecasting is an essential process for estimating future sales and projecting revenue. To achieve more accurate sales predictions, it is recommended to adopt an inductive approach. This involves breaking down sales into smaller components, such as the number of sales visits per day, week, month, or year, and multiplying it by the average number of customers and the average sales value.

For example, let's consider a coffee shop. If the average customer spends $10, and you anticipate serving around 100 customers per day, your daily sales would amount to $1,000. Extrapolating this figure, your projected annual sales would be approximately $350,000.

Sales forecasting is often complemented by cost-of-sales analysis, which helps determine gross profit. By deducting various costs, such as salaries, rent, supplies, and utility bills, from the sales revenue, you can calculate the gross profit of your business.

Accurate sales forecasting and cost analysis enable you to make informed decisions, assess profitability, and plan for future growth. It is important to regularly review and adjust your sales forecast based on market conditions, industry trends, and other relevant factors.

Exercise: Sales Forecast

Year 1 Sales

Product	1	2	3	4	5	6	7	8	9	10	11	12	Annual Sales	Annual Profit
						Months								
a														
b														
Total Sales														
Cost of Sales														
.... expense														
.... expense														
Total Sales														
Gross Profit														

15.3. Startup expenses

Startup expenses refer to the costs that a business incurs before it officially commences operations. These expenses are essential to laying the foundation for the business and preparing it for its launch. During the initial stages, entrepreneurs often face various expenses that are necessary to establish their business identity, infrastructure, and presence in the market.

Some common examples of startup expenses include:

Legal Work: Expenses related to legal consultations, registering the business, obtaining necessary licenses and permits, and drafting contracts or agreements.

Logo Design and Branding: Costs associated with creating a distinctive logo, designing brand elements, and developing a cohesive brand identity.

Marketing Materials: Expenses for producing brochures, business cards, signage, and other promotional materials to create awareness and attract potential customers.

Site Selection and Improvements: Costs involved in finding and securing a suitable location for the business, including lease or rent payments, renovations, and necessary infrastructure setup.

Equipment and Technology: Expenses for purchasing or leasing essential equipment, machinery, tools, and technology systems required to operate the business effectively.

Professional Services: Fees for hiring consultants, accountants, or advisors who provide specialized expertise in areas such as finance, accounting, marketing, or business strategy.

Research and Development: Costs associated with market research, product development, prototype creation, and testing to refine and finalize the business offerings.

Initial Inventory: Expenses for procuring the initial stock or inventory required to start selling products or providing services.

Employee Recruitment and Training: Costs related to the recruitment process, hiring employees, onboarding, and providing initial training.

Insurance and Legal Compliance: Expenses for obtaining business insurance coverage and ensuring compliance with legal and regulatory requirements.

Exercise Startup Expenses
Calculate startup expenses for your business.

Startup Expenses:
Legal Work:
Logo Design and Branding:
Marketing Materials:
Site Selection and Improvements:
Equipment and Technology:
Professional Services:
Research and Development:
Initial Inventory:
Employee Recruitment and Training:
Insurance and Legal Compliance:
Other:

15.4. Startup Assets

Startup assets are the resources and possessions that a business owns and can utilize to generate value. These assets have value and can be converted into cash if needed. In the context of a startup, assets are crucial for establishing and operating the business effectively.

Common examples of startup assets include:

Cash: The available funds that the startup has on hand, which can be used for various purposes such as initial investments, operating expenses, and purchasing other assets.

Equipment: Physical machinery, tools, and devices necessary for the production, manufacturing, or delivery of goods or services. This may include specialized equipment specific to the industry or sector.

Office Furniture and Fixtures: The furniture, fixtures, and fittings required to furnish the office space and create a functional working environment. This can include desks, chairs, cabinets, lighting, and other necessary items.

Computers and Technology: Hardware devices such as computers, laptops, servers, and networking equipment, as well as software applications and systems required for day-to-day operations, data management, and communication.

Machinery and Vehicles: Specific machinery or vehicles used in the production or delivery of goods or services. This can include manufacturing machinery, vehicles for transportation or delivery purposes, or equipment for specialized operations.

Intellectual Property: Intangible assets such as patents, trademarks, copyrights, and trade secrets that provide legal protection and exclusive rights to the startup's innovative ideas, designs, or products.

Inventory: The stock of goods or raw materials that the startup holds for sale or use in its operations. This can include finished products ready for sale, components for production, or supplies necessary for service delivery.

Real Estate or Leasehold Improvements: Physical properties, land, or leasehold improvements made to rented spaces to customize and adapt them to the specific needs of the startup's operations.

Exercise Startup Assets
Calculate startup assets for your business.

Startup Assets:
Cash:
Equipment:
Office furniture and fixtures:
Computers and technology:
Machinery and vehicles:
Intellectual property:
Inventory:
Real estate or leasehold improvements:

Exercise
By using the below table, calculate the total investment requirement.

Total Investment Requirements	
Startup Expenses	
Startup Assets	
Total Investment Requirements	

15.6. Break-Even Analysis

Break-Even Analysis is a financial tool used to determine the point at which a company's total sales revenue equals its total costs, resulting in neither profit nor loss. It helps entrepreneurs predict when their business will start generating a profit.

Every business has fixed costs (such as rent, salaries, and utilities) and variable costs (such as raw materials or production costs). The Break-Even point is reached when the total revenue from sales equals the total costs incurred by the business. At this point, the company is able to cover all its expenses without making a profit or suffering a loss.

The Break-Even analysis is crucial for entrepreneurs as it allows them to make realistic predictions about their net income. It helps them understand how much revenue they need to generate in order to cover their costs and start earning a profit. By identifying the Break-Even point, entrepreneurs can make informed decisions about pricing, production levels, and sales targets to ensure the financial success of their business.

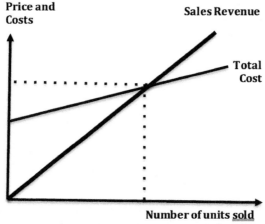

Break-Even Analysis Graphic
Revenues (Sales Income) = Total Costs
at Break-even point

15.7. Total Cost, Variable Cost, and Fixed Cost

Variable costs are expenses that vary in direct proportion to changes in production levels or sales. For example, in a restaurant, the cost of food is a variable cost. As the number of customers increases and more food is served, the cost of food rises accordingly.

On the other hand, fixed costs are expenses that remain relatively constant regardless of sales or output levels. Examples of fixed costs include rent, insurance, and wages. These costs do not fluctuate based on the level of production or sales.

Total cost is the sum of fixed costs and variable costs. It represents the overall cost incurred by a business to produce and sell its products or services. The formula for calculating total cost is:

Total Cost = Fixed Cost + Variable Cost

It is important to note that total costs include some variable costs, as changes in output or sales can impact the overall cost structure of a business. If production levels or sales increase, total costs will also rise. Conversely, if production levels or sales decrease, total costs will decrease as well.

Sales revenue, on the other hand, is the income generated from selling products or services. It is calculated by multiplying the number of units sold by the price of each unit.

Sales Revenue = Sold Units x Sales Price

15.8. Break-Even Analysis Example

ABC Book Store
           Fixed Costs
                     Rent   : $ 4000
Sales Assistant (Wages) : $ 2000
      Total Fixed Cost **: $ 6000**

Variable Costs: **Selling Price:**
  Books: $ 10 per book   Books: $ 20 per book

So we know that:

       Total Fixed Costs = $ 6000
   Variable Cost per Unit = $ 10
   Selling Price per Unit = $ 20

We must first calculate how much income from each book sale can go towards covering the Fixed Costs. This is called the Unit Contribution.

Selling Price - Variable Costs - = Unit Contribution (Profit)
    $ 20 -   10   -   = $ 10

For every book sold, 10 dollars can go towards covering Fixed Costs. Now, let's calculate how many units must be sold to cover Total Costs (FC + VC). It is called the Break-Even Point

Break Even Point (Number of units)= **Fixed Costs** **/** **Unit Contribution (Profit)**
                600 Books = $ 6000   /   10

15.9. Projected Profit and Loss

The Projected Profit and Loss statement, also known as the Income Statement, provides insights into the financial performance of a company by determining whether it is operating at a deficit or generating a profit.

The statement begins with Sales Revenue, which represents the total income generated from the sale of products or services. Direct Costs, also known as Cost of Goods Sold (COGS), are then subtracted from Sales Revenue. This calculation yields the Gross Margin, which is the difference between Sales Revenue and Direct Costs.

It is important to differentiate between the cost of goods and operating expenses. Cost of goods refers to the expense incurred in acquiring or producing the products that are sold. For example, if a product is purchased from a factory for $2 and sold for $3, the direct cost would be $2. Operating expenses, on the other hand, encompass all other expenses not directly associated with the cost of goods sold, such as rent, insurance premiums, and salaries.

Subtracting the operating expenses from the gross margin results in the Gross Profit. Gross Profit is often referred to as EBITDA, which stands for "earnings before interest, taxes, depreciation, and amortization."

The Profit and Loss statement provides a comprehensive view of the financial health of a company by capturing the revenue generated, deducting the costs directly associated with the production or acquisition of goods, and subtracting operating expenses. It helps business owners and stakeholders assess the profitability of the company and make informed decisions to improve financial performance.

| Sales | − | Cost of goods | = | Gross Margin |
| Gross Margin | − | Operation Expenses | = | Gross Profit |

Exercise: Projected Profit and Loss

Months

Year 1	1	2	3	4	5	6	7	8	9	10	11	12
Sales Revenue												
Cost of Goods												
Gross Margin												
Less Op. Exp												
Salaries												
Rent&Utilities												
Advertising												
Sub Total												
Gross Profit												

15.10. Cash Flow Statement

The Cash Flow Statement is a financial statement that provides a summary of the cash and cash equivalents flowing into and out of a company. It offers insights into the operational activities, sources of funds, and expenditures of a business. Additionally, it helps project periods when cash outflows exceed inflows. In situations where the incoming cash is insufficient to cover the outgoing cash, business owners may consider taking a loan to meet their payment obligations. The Cash Flow Statement plays a crucial role in helping investors assess the financial stability of a company.[51]

It's important to note that the Cash Flow Statement does not disclose information about a company's profit or loss; rather, it focuses solely on the company's financial health. Even if a company generates substantial profits, it must effectively manage its cash flow to meet various financial commitments such as salaries, loan repayments, and vendor payments. If a cash flow statement frequently reflects a negative balance, it indicates the need to secure additional investments to address the cash flow issues. Before creating a cash flow projection for your business, it's crucial to identify key assumptions.

These assumptions primarily revolve around receivables and payables. For example, assumptions about receivables would outline the expected speed of customer payments, such as 90% of sales being collected in the month following the sale if most customers pay within 30 days. Similarly, assumptions about payables would define the payment terms with vendors, such as payables being due within 14 days of purchase if vendors require payment within two weeks of delivery.[52] Identifying these key assumptions is vital in creating accurate cash flow projections and effectively managing your company's cash flow.

---

[51] What is Cash Flow Statement, https://www.investopedia.com/investing/what-is-a-cash-flow-statement/#ixzz5lp0HxKBu

[52] Creating a Cash Flow Projection,

https://wellsfargoworks.com/management/article/creating-a-cash-flow-projection

Exercise: Projected Cash Flow

	Month 1	Month 2	Month 3
Beginning Cash Balance			
Sources of Cash			
Receivable Collections			
Customer Deposits			
Loans from the bank			
Other			
Total Sources of Cash			
Uses of Cash			
Payroll and its taxes			
Accounts Payable-Vendors			
Other overhead, Including Rent			
Line of Credit Payments			
Long-Term Principal Payments			
Purchases of Fixed Assets			
Estimated Income Taxes			
Other			
Total Uses of Cash			
Total Sources of Cash			
Total Uses of Cash			
Balance			

15.11. Balance Sheet

The balance sheet provides a snapshot of a company's financial position at a specific moment, encompassing its assets, liabilities, and shareholders' equity. It serves to inform users about the company's financial status by displaying what the company owns and owes.[53]
The structure of a balance sheet aligns with the fundamental accounting equation:
Assets = Liabilities + Owners' Equity
Assets encompass the tangible and intangible possessions of the business that hold monetary value. These include cash, inventory, property, equipment, marketable securities, prepaid expenses, and accounts receivable (money owed to the company by payers). Assets may also encompass intangible assets like patents or trademarks held by the company.
Liabilities represent the monetary obligations and debts owed by the business to external parties. This includes amounts owed on loans, accounts payable, wages, taxes, and other outstanding debts.
Owners' equity reflects the owner's investment in the business, taking into account the owner's initial investment and any subsequent draws made from the business.
By following the equation Assets = Liabilities + Owners' Equity, the balance sheet provides a comprehensive overview of a company's financial standing, allowing stakeholders to assess the value of the company's assets, the extent of its obligations, and the equity held by the owner.

---

[53] Financial Statements 101:

How to Read and Use Your Balance Sheet,
http://www.apapracticecentral.org/business/finances/balance-sheet.aspx

Exercise: Your Balance Sheet, Year 1

Assets		*Capital and Liabilities*	
Cash		**Liabilities**	
Bank balance		Accounts Payable	
Accounts Receivable		Short-term debt	
Inventory		**Total Liabilities**	
		Capital	
		Paid-in Capital	
		Earnings	
Total		**Total**	

16 Business Structure: Choosing the Right Legal Organization Form

Every company has two organizational structures: The formal one is written on the charts; the other is the everyday relationship of the men and women in the organization.
Harold Geneen

16.1. Factors to Consider When Choosing an Organizational Type:

Choosing the right organizational type is a crucial decision for any business. It determines important aspects such as taxation, liability, management structure, continuity, and expenses. Each organizational type has its own advantages and disadvantages, so it's essential to weigh these factors carefully to make an informed choice.

Taxation: The level of taxes paid on profits varies across different organizational types. Some types, such as corporations, have separate tax structures and file taxes independently from personal tax returns.

Liability and Risk: The level of personal liability and the extent of risk exposure differ among organizational types. Certain structures offer limited liability, protecting individuals from personal responsibility in case of harm, property damage, or contract disputes.

Management: Organizational types vary in terms of decision-making authority. Some structures grant individuals full authority and control over decision making, while others require shared decision making and distribution of authority among multiple parties.

Continuity and Transferability: The persistence and saleability of a business can differ based on its organizational type. For example, corporations that issue shares may have greater ease in selling partial ownership stakes.

Expense and Formality: The costs, legal responsibilities, and complexity of establishing and maintaining an organizational type can vary. Some structures have lower startup and ongoing costs and require fewer formalities and legal obligations.

When selecting an organizational type, it is important to carefully consider these factors and assess how they align with your specific business needs, goals, and preferences.

Forms of Legal Organization
There are five common organizational types (also called "legal structures") for small businesses.

- Sole Proprietorship
- Partnership (general, limited, & LLP)
- Limited Liability Company (LLC)
- C-corporation
- S-corporation

16.2. Sole Proprietorship

A Sole Proprietorship is a simple and common form of business ownership where an individual operates and owns the business entirely. As the sole owner, you have complete control and decision-making authority over the business.

Advantages and Disadvantages
- Simplicity and Ease of Setup: Establishing a Sole Proprietorship is relatively straightforward and involves fewer legal formalities and costs compared to other business forms. You can start the business quickly and easily without the need for complex legal documentation or registration processes.
- Direct Control and Decision-Making: As the sole owner, you have full control over all aspects of the business. You can make decisions independently and implement your vision without having to consult or seek approval from others.
- Taxation: One advantage of a Sole Proprietorship is the simplicity of taxation. The business income and expenses are reported on your personal tax return (Schedule C) rather than a separate business tax return. This means that you only pay taxes once on the business profits, avoiding the double taxation that can occur with other forms of business ownership.
- Unlimited Personal Liability: One significant disadvantage of a Sole Proprietorship is that there is no legal distinction between your personal and business assets. As a result, you have unlimited personal liability for the business's debts, obligations, and legal claims. In case of any financial or legal issues, your personal assets may be at risk.
- Limited Ability to Raise Capital: Sole Proprietorships may face challenges in raising capital since the business is solely dependent on the owner's personal funds, savings, or loans. It can be more difficult to attract outside investors or obtain financing compared to other business structures.
- Personal Workload: As the sole owner, you are responsible for all aspects of the business, including day-to-day operations, marketing, financial management, and customer service. This can lead to a heavy workload and limited capacity for growth or expansion without hiring additional staff.

When deciding on a Sole Proprietorship as your organizational form, it is crucial to consider the advantages and disadvantages in relation to your business goals, risk tolerance, and personal circumstances.

16.3. Limited Liability Company (LLC)

A Limited Liability Company (LLC) is a business structure that offers the owners, known as members, limited personal liability for the company's debts and obligations. LLCs combine the benefits of both corporations and partnerships or sole proprietorships. Similar to a corporation, the limited liability feature protects the members' personal assets. Additionally, LLCs provide the advantage of flow-through taxation, where profits and losses are passed through to the members' individual tax returns.

While LLCs offer attractive features, they also have certain disadvantages, particularly in comparison to the structure of a corporation. For example, an LLC must be dissolved upon the death or bankruptcy of a member, unlike a corporation, which can exist indefinitely. Additionally, if the long-term goal is to take the company public, an LLC may not be the most suitable option.

The main reason for choosing an LLC as a business structure is to limit the personal liability of the owners. An LLC is often seen as a combination of a partnership, which is a simple business formation involving two or more owners under an agreement, and a corporation, which provides certain liability protections.

It is important to carefully consider the specific needs and objectives of the business when deciding on the most appropriate organizational structure. Seeking professional advice from legal and financial experts can help in determining whether an LLC is the right choice for your business.

16.4. S Corporation

An S-Corporation is a unique type of corporate entity that provides the owner with the benefits of limited liability, similar to a traditional corporation, while allowing for pass-through taxation, which is characteristic of sole proprietorships or partnerships.

Advantages and Disadvantages

- Similar to C-Corporations: S-Corporations share many of the advantages and characteristics of C-Corporations, including limited liability protection for the owner(s) and the ability to raise capital through the issuance of stock.
- Pass-through Taxation: One significant advantage of an S-Corporation is its pass-through taxation feature. This means that the business's profits and losses are passed through to the owners' personal tax returns, avoiding the double taxation typically associated with C-Corporations.
- Limited Liability: Like a C-Corporation, the owner(s) of an S-Corporation enjoy limited liability protection. This means that their personal assets are generally safeguarded in case of business liabilities or debts.
- Taxation as a Sole Proprietor or Partner: Unlike C-Corporations, where the corporation is taxed as a separate entity, S-Corporation income is treated as personal income for the owner(s). This means that the profits or losses are reported on the owners' individual tax returns, and they are responsible for paying taxes on their share of the income.
- Restrictions and Qualifications: S-Corporations have certain eligibility requirements, such as limitations on the number and type of shareholders, restrictions on the types of stock issued, and residency requirements for shareholders.
- Termination upon Loss of S-Corporation Status: If an S-Corporation no longer meets the eligibility criteria or voluntarily terminates its S-Corporation status, it may be subject to different tax rules and lose the benefits associated with pass-through taxation.

Choosing an S-Corporation as your organizational structure requires careful consideration of its advantages and disadvantages. It is advisable to consult with legal and tax professionals to assess whether an S-Corporation aligns with your business goals, financial situation, and long-term plans.

16.5. C Corporation

A C Corporation is a legal structure for a business entity that provides limited liability protection to its owners, known as shareholders. Unlike an S-Corporation, a C Corporation is not subject to the pass-through taxation feature.

Advantages and Disadvantages
- Limited Liability Protection: One of the primary advantages of a C Corporation is the limited liability protection it offers to its shareholders. The personal assets of the shareholders are generally shielded from business liabilities and debts.
- Ability to Raise Capital: C Corporations have the flexibility to raise capital by issuing different classes of stock, such as common stock and preferred stock. This allows for the attraction of investors and the potential for significant growth.
- Separate Tax Entity: Unlike an S-Corporation, which passes through its income to the owners' personal tax returns, a C Corporation is a separate tax entity. It files its own tax return and is subject to corporate tax rates. This can result in potential double taxation, as the corporation's profits are taxed at the corporate level and any dividends distributed to shareholders are taxed at the individual level.
- Perpetual Existence: A C Corporation has perpetual existence, meaning it continues to exist even if there are changes in ownership or management. This offers stability and continuity for the business.
- Flexibility in Ownership: C Corporations allow for a broad range of ownership, including both domestic and foreign shareholders. There are no restrictions on the number of shareholders or the types of stock issued. Complexity and Compliance: Compared to other business structures, C Corporations typically have more complex legal and compliance requirements. This includes adhering to corporate formalities, maintaining accurate financial records, holding regular shareholder meetings, and filing annual reports. Tax Planning
- Opportunities: C Corporations offer tax planning opportunities through deductible expenses, employee benefits, and retirement plans. They may also have the ability to retain earnings and reinvest in the business at a potentially lower tax rate.

Choosing a C Corporation as your organizational structure requires careful consideration of its advantages and disadvantages. It is advisable to consult with legal, tax, and financial professionals to assess whether a C Corporation aligns with your business goals, financial situation, and long-term plans.

Exercise: What Will Be Your Organizational Form?

Choosing the organizational form for your business is a critical decision that requires careful consideration of the pros and cons associated with each option. While Sole Proprietorship and LLC are popular choices for many entrepreneurs, it's important to assess which form aligns best with your specific needs and goals.

Sole Proprietorship offers simplicity and ease of setup, as it does not require any formal registration or separate taxation. However, it also means that you have unlimited personal liability for the business's debts and obligations. This form is typically suitable for small, low-risk businesses with minimal regulatory requirements.

On the other hand, an LLC provides the advantages of limited liability, separating personal and business assets, and potential tax benefits. It offers a more formal structure and provides a sense of credibility to your business. Additionally, an LLC allows for flexibility in management and the potential for growth and expansion.

Considering that the term "startup" implies growth potential, an LLC may be a more favorable choice. However, the final decision depends on your specific circumstances, such as the nature of your business, your risk tolerance, the desire for personal asset protection, and the long-term vision for your company.

17 The End Game: Planning for Succession and Exit Strategies in Business

Do you want to know who you are? Don't ask. Act! Action will delineate and define you."
Thomas Jefferson

17.1. Why do we need an exit strategy?

An exit strategy is a crucial component for entrepreneurs and investors, particularly those involved in startup companies, as it provides a means to transfer ownership or recoup investments. It differs significantly between small businesses and startups. While small business owners often focus on generating income and aim to sustain their business indefinitely, startup founders prioritize creating value and envision a grand exit strategy.

The ultimate goal of any business venture is to generate income. A small bookstore, for example, aims to achieve high revenues and profits as quickly as possible to fuel growth. On the other hand, a startup in the health and lifestyle industry may amass a million subscribers without earning any direct revenue. However, the substantial user base holds significant value, and the startup founder can capitalize on this value by selling the company at a high price.

Not only startup founders but also investors seek to realize their returns. The increase in value for a startup may be independent of revenue and profits. Companies like Hotmail, Facebook, or WhatsApp had minimal income during their initial years. However, they demonstrated their ability to create substantial value for users, and the market recognized this value, which attracted investors eager to acquire these companies. When the market is ready to purchase the value created by the startup, the founder can consider various exit alternatives. An exit strategy is typically executed when predetermined criteria for profitability have been met or exceeded.

There are several exit strategies available, and they can vary significantly between startups and small businesses. Small businesses may opt for liquidation or succession as their exit strategy. In contrast, startups may consider options such as an initial public offering (IPO), management buyout, mergers, or acquisitions to facilitate their exit from the market. Each strategy offers unique advantages and considerations, and selecting the most suitable approach depends on the specific circumstances and goals of the business.

In conclusion, having a well-defined exit strategy is essential for entrepreneurs and investors. It ensures a smooth transition of ownership and allows for the realization of investments. Understanding the different exit strategies available and tailoring them to the specific nature of the business is crucial for maximizing value and achieving a successful exit.

17.2. Exit Strategies

Merger & Acquisition (M&A):
A merger occurs when two companies join forces and combine their resources and complementary skills to form a single entity. On the other hand, acquisition refers to a larger company purchasing a startup to leverage the capabilities and assets of the acquired company. Notable examples include Facebook's acquisition of WhatsApp and Google's acquisition of YouTube. M&A is considered one of the most effective exit strategies for startups.

Initial Public Offering (IPO):
An IPO involves taking a startup public by listing and selling its shares on the stock market. Going public through an IPO is a dream for many startups, although it is relatively rare. Startups funded by experienced investors with IPO expertise may have a higher chance of successfully going public. Choosing an IPO as an exit strategy requires a strong public relations strategy, a reputable brand image, and significant media presence. This option is particularly viable for startups with groundbreaking technologies or services that attract widespread attention.

Sell to a Friendly Buyer:
Selling the company to a friendly buyer can be a favorable exit alternative. Starting a business and growing it are two distinct skill sets. As a founder, you may excel at initiating the business but lack expertise in successfully scaling and managing it. Selling to an investor or buyer who has the capacity and skills to nurture the business's growth can be an ideal fit. The buyer's willingness to pay for the firm will be based on its potential income and revenues, recognizing the growth opportunities that lie ahead.

Turn Your Business into Your Cash Cow:
If your company generates a steady revenue stream and provides returns to investors, you have the option to hire someone you trust to run the business while you retain ownership. This allows you to enjoy annual income from the business while continuing your entrepreneurial journey.

Management Buyout (MBO):
A management buyout involves selling the company to its existing managers. The management team possesses deep knowledge of the business, clients, financials, and company culture. As insiders, they can expedite the due diligence process and evaluation of the firm. The management team's belief in the company's potential motivates them to purchase it. Financing for the buyout can be obtained through bank loans or by involving private equity investors.

Liquidation:
Liquidation involves converting assets into cash by selling them directly. Liquidation prospects differ across industries. Service-based businesses like law or insurance have limited liquidation value due to the limited worth of office furniture and equipment. However, restaurants, retail stores, and other businesses with physical inventory may have better liquidation potential, especially if they can transfer the location rights. Retail inventory can be sold online or through physical stores, allowing the startup owner to recoup some value from their remaining stock.

When choosing an exit strategy, it is crucial to carefully assess the specific circumstances, financial position, and long-term objectives of the business.

Epilogue

Now, It's Your Turn.

From that initial spark of an idea to a well-defined business niche, I have walked with you in the pages of this book. We've mulled over choosing the right business idea, dived deep into understanding your target customers, built a robust business model, and strategized on standing out in the market.

You have explored the art of starting lean, developing a strong brand, and effectively reaching your audience. You have cracked the code of hiring and keeping the right team, delivering a persuasive business pitch, and making sense of financial forecasting. And at the end, you have navigated the legal aspects of setting up your business.

But let me be honest. This book doesn't have all the answers. No book does. The business landscape is always changing, throwing up new challenges and opportunities. This playbook is a starting point, a basecamp. The real adventure begins when you step out, applying what you've learned and improvising when you need to.

Embrace the unknown and the unexpected. See hurdles not as roadblocks but as chances to innovate and grow. Stay resilient because things won't always go as planned.

Building relationships matters as much as building your business. Nurture your connections—they are your most valuable resource. Learn from others, seek advice, share your journey, and celebrate the successes together.

Hold onto that passion that set you off on this journey in the first place. Feed it, fuel it. Let it light up those long nights and early mornings. Remember, every stumble, every win, and even every dead-end are part of the journey.

Launching or growing a business isn't just about making money. It's about making your mark.

This is your beginning. Now, take a deep breath, gear up, and step into your new adventure.

Special Thanks

First off, I've got to tip my hat to my professors at NYU and Harvard, and an outstanding teacher Ahmet Aksoy. You taught me more than business strategies—you showed me how to navigate life. Thank you for sowing the seeds of entrepreneurship in my mind and heart.

Mom, Dad—thank you doesn't even begin to cover it. From the first book stand to this latest venture, you've been my constant support Your belief in me, even when I was a teen with crazy ideas, has been a lifeline. Your love and encouragement prepared me for these days.

To my clients, you've trusted me with your businesses, and I can't thank you enough. Our training sessions, our deep discussions and workshop—they've all helped me grow, pushing me to learn more,.

My brilliant students—you make me proud, every single day. You might think I taught you, but you taught me so much more. You filled our classrooms with energy and innovation, constantly keeping me on my toes.

And finally, to my family. You're my rock, my sanctuary. I've lost count of the dinners I missed, the bedtime stories I couldn't read because I was burning the midnight oil. But you understood. You stood by me, and you loved me even when I was a grumpy mess. I owe you everything.

Wrapping this up, I know how rich my journey has been, filled with people who've shaped me, supported me. This book isn't just about my passion for entrepreneurship—it's a tribute to all the beautiful friends and fox who've been a part of my personal discoveries.

Sources

Ackoff, Russel L. "Mission statements." Planning Review (1987).

Adom, Alex Yaw, Israel Kofi Nyarko, and Gladys Narki Kumi Som. "Competitor analysis in strategic management: Is it a worthwhile managerial practice in contemporary times." Journal of Resources Development and Management 24.1 (2016): 116-127.

Alan Gleeson, The Business Pitch, **http://articles.bplans.co.uk/starting-a-business/the-business-pitch/407**.

Christensen, Clayton M., Scott Cook, and Taddy Hall. "What customers want from your products." Harvard Business School Newsletter: Working Knowledge (2006).

Cooper, Robert G. "How new product strategies impact on performance." Journal of Product Innovation Management 1.1 (1984): 5-18.

Crosling, M. (2023, February 14). Know the Difference Between Features and Benefits. Retrieved June 8, 2023, from **https://strategiccontent.co/difference-between-features-and-benefits/**.

Davila, Antonio, and George Foster. "Management control systems in early-stage startup companies." The accounting review 82.4 (2007): 907-937.

Dell, Michael. Direct from Dell: Strategies that revolutionized an industry. SAGE Publications, 2002.

Dontchev, Asen L., R. Tyrrell Rockafellar, and R. Tyrrell Rockafellar. Implicit functions and solution mappings: A view from variational analysis. Vol. 11. New York: Springer, 2009.

Elgendy, Mostafa, Cecilia Sik-Lanyi, and Arpad Kelemen. "Making shopping easy for people with visual impairment using mobile assistive technologies." Applied Sciences 9.6 (2019): 1061.

Eric Ries, The Lean Startup, Currency, 2011.

Fleisher, Craig S., and Babette E. Bensoussan. Business and competitive analysis: effective application of new and classic methods. FT press, 2015.

Ford, David. "Develop your technology strategy." Long range planning 21.5 (1988): 85-95.

Frank Robinson, A Proven Methodology to Maximize Return on Risk, 2001, **http://www.syncdev.com/minimum-viable-product/**.

Frederick, Howard, Donald Kuratko, and Allan O'Connor. Entrepreneurship: Theory/Process/Practice. 4th ed., Cengage Learning, 2016, p. 54.

Freeman, Christopher. "The determinants of innovation: Market demand, technology, and the response to social problems." Futures 11.3 (1979): 206-215.

Getzels, Jacob W., and Mihaly Csikszentmihalyi. "From problem solving to problem finding." Perspectives in creativity. Routledge, 2017. 90-116.

James Bethell, Body Shop changes strategy on public relations, **https://www.independent.co.uk/news/business/body-shop-changes-strategy-on-public-relations-1442891.html**.

Kadile, Vita, and Alessandro Biraglia. "From hobby to business: Exploring environmental antecedents of entrepreneurial alertness using fsQCA." Journal of Small Business Management 60.3 (2022): 580-615.

Kapella, Victor. "A framework for incident and problem management." International Network Services whitepaper (2003).

Karmarkar, Uma R., Baba Shiv, and Brian Knutson. "Cost conscious? The neural and behavioral impact of price primacy on decision making." Journal of Marketing Research 52.4 (2015): 467-481.

Kim, Bohyun. "Gamification." Library Technology Reports 51.2 (2015): 10-18.

Levin, Ira M. "Vision revisited: Telling the story of the future." The Journal of Applied Behavioral Science 36.1 (2000): 91-107.

Market Definition, Conceptual Diagram, NetMBA, **http://www.netmba.com/marketing/market/definition**, retrieved on June 8, 2023.

McLeod, Stephen. "Absolute biological needs." Bioethics 28.6 (2014): 293-301.

Mühlhäuser, Max. "Smart products: An introduction." Constructing Ambient Intelligence: AmI 2007 Workshops Darmstadt, Germany, November 7-10, 2007 Revised Papers. Springer Berlin Heidelberg, 2008.

Olsen, Dan. The Lean Product Playbook: How to Innovate with Minimum Viable Products and Rapid Customer Feedback, 2015, pg. 90.

Osterwalder, Alexander, et al. "Business model generation." Business Model (2005).

Osterwalder, Alexander, et al. Value proposition design: How to create products and services customers want. John Wiley & Sons, 2015.

Pehrsson, Anders. "Barriers to entry and market strategy: a literature review and a proposed model." European Business Review 21.1 (2009): 64-77.

Ries, Al, and Jack Trout. Positioning: The Battle for Your Mind. 20th anniversary ed., McGraw-Hill, 2001.

Sampson Quain, Examples of Corporate Philosophy, **http://smallbusiness.chron.com/examples-corporate-philosophy-37868.html**.

Sengupta, Sanjit. "Some approaches to complementary product strategy." Journal of Product Innovation Management: AN INTERNATIONAL PUBLICATION OF THE PRODUCT DEVELOPMENT & MANAGEMENT ASSOCIATION 15.4 (1998): 352-367.

Seybold, Patricia B. "Get inside the lives of your customers." Harvard Business Review 79.5 (2001): 80-9.

Simonton, Dean Keith. "Scientific creativity: Discovery and invention as combinatorial." Frontiers in Psychology 12 (2021): 721104.

Smith, Tim. Pricing strategy: Setting price levels, managing price discounts and establishing price structures. Cengage Learning, 2011.

Stampfl, Georg, Reinhard Prügl, and Vincent Osterloh. "An explorative model of business model scalability." International Journal of Product Development 18.3-4 (2013): 226-248.

Steve Johnson, What you didn't know about Apple's '1984' Super Bowl ad, **http://www.chicagotribune.com/entertainment/tv/ct-apple-1984-ad-myths-ent-0205-20170201-column.html**.

Talluri, Srinivas, and Ram Narasimhan. "A methodology for strategic sourcing." European journal of operational research 154.1 (2004): 236-250.

Tang, Jintong, K. Michele Micki Kacmar, and Lowell Busenitz. "Entrepreneurial alertness in the pursuit of new opportunities." Journal of business venturing 27.1 (2012): 77-94.

Tynan, Caroline, and Sally McKechnie. "Experience marketing: a review and reassessment." Journal of marketing management 25.5-6 (2009): 501-517.

What is Cash Flow Statement, **https://www.investopedia.com/investing/what-is-a-cash-flow-statement/#ixzz5Ip0HxKBu**.

Whole Foods Core Values, **https://www.wholefoodsmarket.com/mission-values/core-values**.

Woźniak, Dariusz, and Sokołowska-Woźniak, Justyna. Innovation, Entrepreneurship and Psychological Traits as Factors Influencing Productivity. Polonya, Fundation for the Dissemination of Knowledge and Science "Cognitione", 2018.

Printed in Great Britain
by Amazon

23932255R00106